# BEAUTIFUL QUILTAGAMI

# BEAUTIFUL QUILTAGAMI

## NEW IDEAS
## FOR FABRIC FOLDING

## MARY JO HINEY

STERLING PUBLISHING CO., INC. NEW YORK
A STERLING/CHAPELLE BOOK

CHAPELLE, LTD.

Jo Packham • Sara Toliver • Cindy Stoeckl

Editor: Karmen Quinney

Copy Editor: Marilyn Goff

Graphic Illustrator: Kim Taylor

Art Director: Karla Haberstich

Photography: Ryne Hazen for Hazen Photography

Photo Stylist: Suzy Skadburg

Staff: Kelly Ashkettle • Anne Bruns • Areta Bingham
Donna Chambers • Emily Frandsen •
Susan Jorgensen • Jennifer Luman • Melissa Maynard
Barbara Milburn • Lecia Monsen • Desirée Wybrow

Library of Congress Cataloging-in-Publication Data Available

Hiney, Mary Jo
  Beautiful quiltagami: new idea for fabric folding/
Mary Jo Hiney.
    p. cm.
  "A Sterling/Chapelle Book."
  Includes index.
  ISBN 1-4027-0938-2
1. Patchwork--Pattern.  2. Origami.  3. Quilting.  I Title.
TT835.H45822  2004
746.46--dc22                           2004009148

10 9 8 7 6 5 4 3 2 1

Published by Sterling Publishing Co., Inc.
387 Park Avenue South, New York, NY 10016
©2004 by Mary Jo Hiney
Distributed in Canada by Sterling Publishing
℅ Manda Group, 165 Dufferin Street
Toronto, Ontario, Canada M6K 3H6
Distributed in Great Britain by Chrysalis Books Group PLC, The
Chrysalis Building, Bramley Road, London W10 6SP, England
Distributed in Australia by Capricorn Link (Australia) Pty. Ltd.
P.O. Box 704, Windsor, NSW 2756, Australia
Printed in the USA
All Rights Reserved

Sterling ISBN 1-4027-0938-2

Due to the limited amount of space available, we must print our patterns at a reduced size in order to give our patrons the maximum number of patterns possible in our publications. We believe the quality and quantity of our patterns will compensate for any inconvenience this may cause.

Space would not permit the inclusion of every decorative item photographed for this book, nor could all of the designers be identified. Many of these items are available by calling:
  Ruby & Begonia
  204 25th Street, Ogden, UT 84401
  (801) 334-7829 or(888) 888-7829 Toll-free
  e-mail: ruby@rubyandbegonia.com
  Web site: www.rubyandbegonia.com

WRITE US

If you have questions or comments, please contact:
  Chapelle, Ltd., Inc.,
  P.O. Box 9252, Ogden, UT 84409
  (801) 621-2777 • (801) 621-2788 Fax
  e-mail: chapelle@chapelleltd.com
  Web site: chapelleltd.com

Resources for Origami Folds:

Super Simple Origami, by Irmgard Kneissler, 1999, Sterling Publishing, New York,

Beautiful Origami, by Zulal Ayture-Scheele, 1990, Sterling Publishing, New Yor

A Butterfly for Alice Gray, by Michael la Fosse, 1994, http://dev.origami.com

Continuous Prairie Points technique with special thanks for instructions to Marinda Stewart

Overlapped and Entwined element variations adaptation from: Square Box, New World Origami Series: Book 1, by Tomoko Fuse, http://www.owt.com/gdscott

The Joy of Origami, by Toshie Takahama, 1985, Shufunotomo Co., Ltd., Tokyo, Japan

# TABLE OF CONTENTS

# GENERAL INSTRUCTIONS

Quiltagami is the art of folding and sewing fabric—origami style. The folded and sewn fabric is then assembled into blocks for quilting.

Quilters and origami enthusiasts have an opportunity once again, with Mary Jo Hiney's second Quiltagami book, to merge the two art forms into an altogether new textile art.

The traditions of beautiful fabric selections in harmonizing patterns and colors, accurate sewing, and the meticulous assembly and finishing techniques of quilting are paired with the precise valley- and mountain-folding techniques of origami figures. This book offers step-by-step colored folding diagrams for all of the quiltagami projects.

Bead and ribbon embellishments add exquisite detail to folded and sewn quiltagami figures. With Mary Jo's instructions and examples, the quilter's scrap box and imagination are resources for an entirely new fabric art form.

## STANDARD TOOLS & NOTIONS

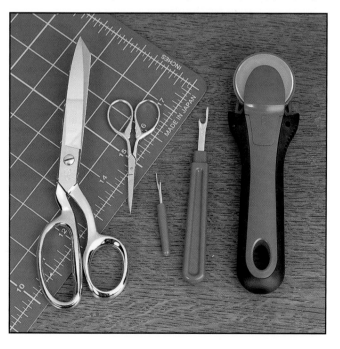

Following are supplies that every quilter should have on hand before beginning, along with required fabrics and notions for each project. Remember to press every seam once before proceeding with the next step. Match all intersecting seams.

- #2 pencil
- Copier paper
- Disappearing-ink fabric marker
- Fabric scissors
- Fine-tipped permanent ink fabric marker
- Fray preventative
- Hand-sewing needles
- Iron/ironing board
- Neutral shades of thread
- Permanent ink gel pens
- Quilter's ruler
- Quilting needles
- Quilting pins
- Rotary cutter
- Seam ripper
- Self-healing cutting mat
- Sewing machine
- Sewing-machine needles
- Spray bottle/water
- Spray starch
- Tape measure
- Tracing paper
- Water-soluble fabric marker

# FABRIC PRINTING TOOLS

Following are supplies that will aid in printing lettering onto fabric:

- Computer with image-editing software and printer, or copier (at home or copy shop)

- Deckle-edged scissors

- Hard flat pressing surface such as a piece of particle board

- Ink-jet transfer paper for use with ink-jet printer

- Letters, poems, or prose

- Press cloth

- Silicon press sheet

- Vellum tracing paper

# PILLOW TOOLS & NOTIONS

Following are supplies that will be used to create each pillow front:

- Assortment of beading, embroidery, and hand-sewing needles

- Grid-lined ruler

## TIP:

Make the back of the pillow attractive so that you can display both sides.

# BASIC QUILTAGAMI

For practicing purposes, all you need is an 8½"-square piece of fabric or sheet of paper. However, practicing with both fabric and paper can best help you achieve your Quiltagami goals. Paper folding provides very obvious lines that help as you proceed with each step. Fabric, besides being wonderful and the purpose of Quiltagami, is different to work with than paper in that it is very pliable and cooperative.

A good way to try out a technique is by first folding it from paper. When you then try the design with fabric, you can refer to the paper folded piece and you will notice the cooperation of the fabric. Familiarize yourself with the basics of origami, as the folding basics are essential bits of information.

There are three main Quiltagami issues to be resolved when working with fabric: 1) multiple fabric folds create bulk, 2) multiple fabric folds tend to cause a design element to get lost within the layers and, of course, 3) fabric has raw edges that fray. These three main issues are resolved within each Quiltagami technique. The most dynamic issue resolved involves making certain that design elements are maintained. This is accomplished by piecing a contrasting fabric to a square before folding begins. The contrasting fabric forces the eye to notice the difference, which helps our brain to acknowledge the entire folded creation.

There are two materials that can make a world of difference in your Quiltagami fabric folding. 1) Spray starch will make specific creases very crisp and add to the overall dimensionality of a design. 2) Fray preventative can be used to eliminate fabric fraying in areas that are just too tiny to make a finished edge. Keep these two items handy.

Several Quiltagami designs can be created from the same basic forms, which are made up of a common set of preliminary folds. These basic forms are used throughout the projects in this book.

## CREASING TOOLS FOR PAPER

**Fingers** are excellent for making sharp creases. Pinch fabric crease lightly between thumbnail and forefinger at end of fold and move along the edge of the fold to make a sharp clean crease. This comes in handy with relaxing an open crease. You can also create a sharp crease by laying the folded fabric on a hard flat surface and running your middle finger and forefinger along the edge of the fold.

**Wooden skewers** come in handy for gently pushing folded corners and points out. Wooden skewers become especially useful when folding tiny pieces of Quiltagami.

## CREASING TOOLS & AIDS FOR FABRIC

**Ironing** is a fast and easy method to fold fabrics into crisp Quiltagami shapes. I prefer to use a standard-sized iron with Quiltagami techniques, but an appliqué iron will work in a pinch.

**Fabric starches** come in sprays and are used to make fabrics easier to handle as well as maintaining a crisp crease.

**Straight pins** are handy to hold corners or folds in place while pressing fabric folds with an iron. They are useful in keeping fingertips away from the iron.

# BASIC SYMBOLS FOR FOLDING TECHNIQUE DIRECTIONS

Symbols are used in the folding steps to indicate a forthcoming action. The symbols will be placed on the diagram. Please review the following symbols before beginning the projects in this book. Paper instead of fabric has been used in the photos to better illustrate the creases and folding techniques.

## FOLD IN FRONT & VALLEY FOLD

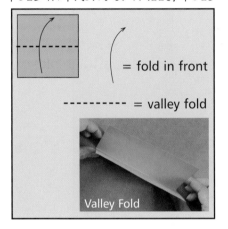

= fold in front

---------- = valley fold

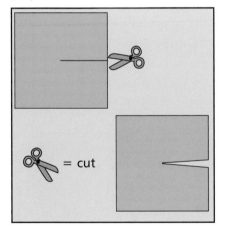

Valley Fold

## FOLD BEHIND & MOUNTAIN FOLD

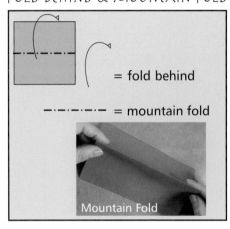

= fold behind

—·—·—·— = mountain fold

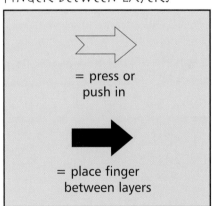

Mountain Fold

## CREASE, OR FOLD & UNFOLD

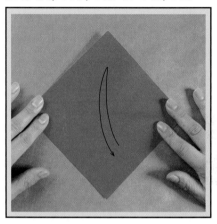

## CUT

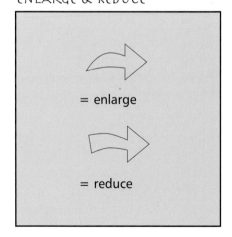

= cut

## PRESS OR PUSH IN & PLACE FINGER BETWEEN LAYERS

= press or push in

= place finger between layers

## ENLARGE & REDUCE

= enlarge

= reduce

## TURN MODEL OVER

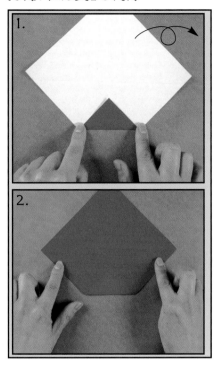

## ROTATE THE MODEL, INFLATE & INSERT OR PULL OUT

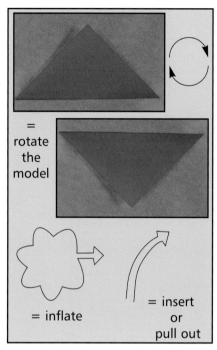

= rotate the model

= inflate

= insert or pull out

## INSIDE REVERSE FOLD

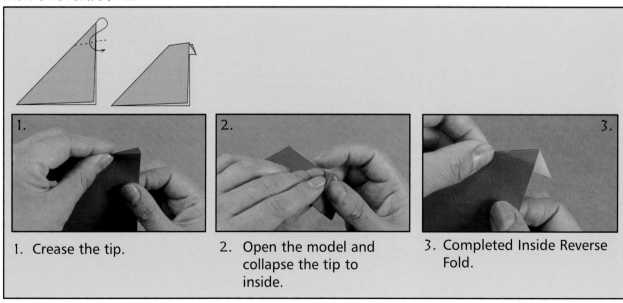

1. Crease the tip.

2. Open the model and collapse the tip to inside.

3. Completed Inside Reverse Fold.

## FOLD OVER & FOLD BACK, OR PLEAT FOLD

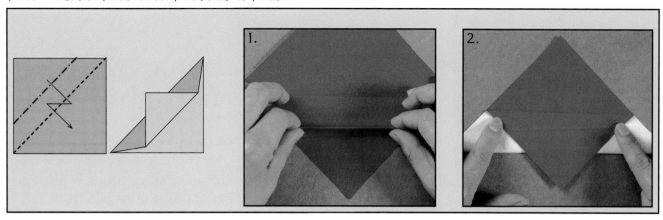

## OUTSIDE REVERSE FOLD

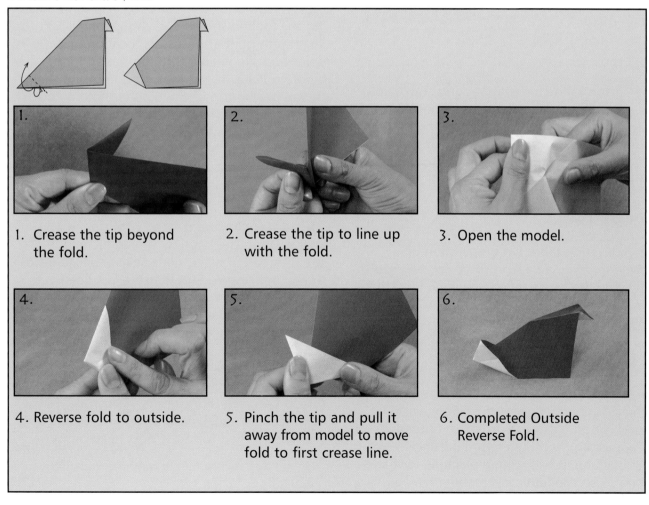

1. Crease the tip beyond the fold.

2. Crease the tip to line up with the fold.

3. Open the model.

4. Reverse fold to outside.

5. Pinch the tip and pull it away from model to move fold to first crease line.

6. Completed Outside Reverse Fold.

# BASIC QUILTING ELEMENTS

## APPLIQUÉ

Stitch elements in place on a quilt front with a single strand of floss or doubled thread and hand-sewing needle of choice. I prefer to use a fine embroidery needle because I like the length of the needle, sharpness of the point, and larger needle eye. Use small whipstitches to stitch an edge in place.

## BACKING

Use cotton fabric for quilt backing. You can create a randomly pieced backing from the remaining fabric scraps you have purchased for the quilt front. The pieced quilt backing need not have a pattern—it simply needs to be the right size.

## BASTING SPRAY

When layering fabrics in preparation of machine-quilting, a basting spray can be used to lightly glue the layers together, eliminating the need for pinning. The basting spray will wash out with laundering.

## BATTING

Batting is used as the middle layer of a quilt. There are numerous types of batting available. Bonded cotton batting gives a flat, natural appearance and is the preferred batting to use for Quiltagami. It will require machine- or hand-quilting to secure fabric layers together.

## BEADING

Use doubled thread to stitch beads in place on a quilt front. Several different needle types can be used for this task. The obvious choice is the beading needle and for some beads, it is the only needle that will slide through a bead hole. Other needle choices include a very fine embroidery needle and a milliner's needle. Try either as a needle option.

To begin beading in a knotless fashion, slip both thread ends through the needle eye, having the looped thread end as the longer length. Stitch into quilt at necessary location or entry point and slip needle through thread loop before pulling thread taut, thus knotting the thread on the top of the quilt without a knot. Slip needle through bead and position bead at thread entry point. Stitch back into quilt at opposite end of bead, then stitch thread through the quilt top layer and back to the original entry point. Restitch bead in place a second time.

**Bead dangles** are created with thread and beads. Using the knotless thread technique, stitch thread in place. Slide several beads onto thread, making certain that the last bead is a seed bead. Stitch back through all the beads, except the last seed bead that was placed on the needle. Wiggle and pull thread through beads while also moving beads to thread entry point. Stitch back into fabric at entry point and make a very small knot with the thread. Move thread between fabric layers, if possible, to the next beading spot. Make a very small knot with the thread, then form the next bead dangle.

## BINDING

To bind a quilt, cut a straight piece of fabric that is the length of the edge to be finished plus 1½". Width can vary according to desired binding size. For ¼" finished binding, cut strips that are 1⅝" wide. For ½" binding, cut strips that are 2⅝" wide. If necessary, piece lengths together by first diagonally cutting the ends to be pieced, then sewing ends, using ¼" seam allowance. Press the length in half, matching the long edges. Align the long raw edges with the quilt edge and sew layers together, using ¼" seam allowance. Press binding outward, then fold it around to the back side. Position the folded edge of the binding over the binding seam line and stitch or machine-sew the binding in place. When necessary, fold ends under before folding binding around to the back side.

## FABRICS

The fabrics used for Quiltagami techniques are primarily quilting cottons. For some of the projects, silk organza or dupioni has been used in Quiltagami techniques. Cottons, silks, and wools have been used to create the projects. Natural fibers are manageable to work with and press well. Cotton fabrics should be prewashed before assembling the quilts or Quiltagami techniques.

**Cutting fabrics** the correct way is very important. When cutting squares for folding, accuracy and cutting on the grain are important. Use a quilter's ruler, a self-healing cutting mat and a rotary cutter to cut accurately straight and a square pieces of fabric. Use the cutting mat and rotary cutter to trim fabric pieces to size within the process of creating a project.

## FREE-MOTION QUILTING

For machine-quilting, replace presser foot with a darning foot. Refer to sewing machine manufacturer's directions for proper installation of the darning foot, etc. Lower the feed dogs. With quilt in place under darning foot, begin sewing, moving the quilt around in a random or planned design.

## LAYERING BACKING, BATTING & QUILT FRONT

Place the backing fabric on floor or work table, wrong side up. Place the batting over the backing. Place the quilt front over the batting, right side up. The layers can be held together using basting spray, straight pins, safety pins, or hand-basting stitches.

## LIGHTWEIGHT FUSIBLE KNIT INTER-FACING

Use this type of interfacing when fabric needs a little more body without becoming stiff.

# FOUNDATION PIECING

Foundation fabrics must be stable enough to stitch fabric pieces onto, and sheer enough to see through. The best example of a foundation fabric is lightweight nonwoven interfacing that is nonfusible. Purchase the very lightest weight you can find. Using a fine-tipped permanent ink fabric marker, trace directly onto the interfacing. As the interfacing is very lightweight, it adds little bulk to a foundation-pieced quilt block or project and eliminates the need to tear away foundation-piecing paper. It is a bit of a nuisance to trace onto the nonwoven interfacing, but not nearly as much of an ordeal as tearing paper away from a sewn block. Other examples of foundation fabrics are muslin, paper, and tear-away backing. A non-tear-away foundation fabric will add an extra piece of fabric to quilt through. You may wish to experiment to discover your preferred foundation material.

Foundation piecing often requires preseaming. Preseaming means that two pieces of fabric may need to be stitched together before being stitched onto the foundation. The fabrics must be cut to the shape of the area and sewn together. They are then treated as one unit, with the seam resting on the appropriate seam line. Except when preseaming is required, fabric pieces need not be cut perfectly. Use strips, rectangles, squares, or any other odd-shaped scrap material.

Make certain fabric is at least ⅜" larger on all sides than the area it is to cover. As triangular shapes are more difficult to piece, use generously sized fabric pieces and position pieces carefully on the foundation. Some fabric is wasted in foundation piecing, but the time saved is well worth the results. Through practice, you will discover the most effective and least wasteful sizes to cut fabric pieces.

## FOUNDATION PIECING INSTRUCTIONS

Note: If necessary, make certain to enlarge pattern to required percentage on photocopier.

1. Transfer pattern onto foundation. Using fine-tipped permanent ink fabric marker or #2 pencil, write all numbers on foundation.

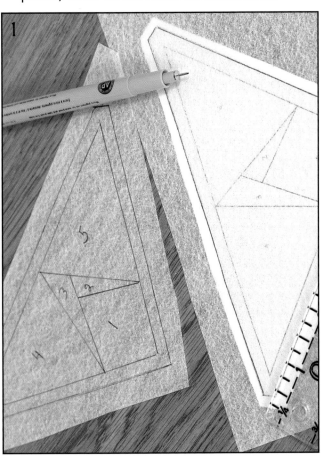

2. Cut fabric piece for block. When making many blocks, make a chart as an aid to note fabrics, number placements, cut sizes, and quantities needed for each fabric.

3. Turn over foundation with unmarked side up. Place fabric piece 1, right side up, on shape 1. If foundation is not sheer, hold foundation up to a light source to make certain that fabric overlaps at least ¼" on all sides of shape 1. Pin, glue, or hold in place.

4. Make certain that fabric piece 2 overlaps at least ¼" on all sides of shape 2. Place fabric piece 2 on fabric piece 1, right sides together.

5. Turn over foundation, with marked side up. Sew along line between shapes 1 and 2, using a very small stitch. Note: This is helpful if paper has been used as the foundation. Begin and end two or three stitches beyond the line.

6. Trim excess fabric ⅛"–¼" past seam line. Take care not to cut foundation.

7. Turn over foundation, with unmarked side up. Open fabric piece 2 and finger-press seam. Pin or glue in place, if necessary.

8. Make certain that fabric piece 3 overlaps at least ¼" on all sides of shape 3. Place fabric piece 3 on fabric piece 1, with right sides together. Secure in place. Repeat Steps 5–6 on opposite page and above.

9. Press once all pieces have been sewn in place on a unit. Stitch ⅛" inward from outer edge of foundation's seam allowance. Trim the foundation unit on seam line. Assemble units as directed.

## GENERAL QUILTAGAMI TIPS:

• Remove batting from the package a day before using. Open it out to full size. This will help the batting to lie flat.

• Test elements and fabrics by placing them onto the backdrop fabric. The more elements that you can see together at one time, the better able you will be to make final decisions about fabric choices. Once you are pleased with your colorations and fabrics, begin to assemble the project as instructed.

• Use tiny stitches when sewing circles.

• Remember to make the back side of quilt attractive as well. See photo below.

# GEOMETRIC-FOLD QUILT

## FABRICS:

Note: All fabrics are a minimum of 42" wide.

### Cool (two variations)
- Aqua print (½ yd) for Block 1
- Yellow/lime striped (½ yd) for Block 1

### Coral (three variations)
- Coral burst (1¼ yd) for Blocks 1, 2, and 3
- Coral swirl (½ yd) for Block 1
- Coral/yellow floral (½ yd) for Blocks 2 and 3

### Gold (two variations)
- Curry solid (1¼ yd) for Blocks 2, 3, and 4
- Pale gold tone-on-tone (½ yd) for binding

### Ivory (three variations)
- Ivory broadcloth solid (1¼ yd) for Blocks 1 and 4
- Ivory floral print (½ yd) for Blocks 1 and 4
- Ivory patterned print (½ yd) for Block 1

### Pink (four variations)
- Dark pink plaid (½ yd) for Blocks 2 and 3
- Fuchsia print (½ yd) for Blocks 1 and 4
- Pink plaid (½ yd) for Blocks 2 and 3
- Pink variegated (½ yd) for Block 3

### Terra-cotta (three variations)
- Terra-cotta plaid (1¼ yd) for Blocks 2, 3, and 4
- Terra-cotta/gold variegated (½ yd) for Blocks 2, 3, and 4
- Terra-cotta textured (½ yd) for Block 3

## NOTIONS:
- **Standard Tools & Notions** on page 8
- Cotton batting
- Quilt basting spray

## DEFINING THE PROJECT

Four different geometric-fold techniques, presented in four different traditionally inspired quilt blocks are used for this bold geometric quilt. The quilt requires thirteen of Block 1, five of Block 2, seven of Block 3, and forty-four of Block 4.

## CREATING BLOCK 1

Folding technique: Overlapping & Entwined
    Triangles: Folded Over

Finished size: 10" square

Note: Enlarge pattern 200% unless otherwise
indicated.

1. Using **Triangle A** pattern on page 27, cut triangle from each of the following fabrics:
   - four from aqua print or yellow/lime striped
   - two from coral burst
   - two from coral swirl

2. Cut one 1¾" x 23" strip from each of the
   following fabrics:
   - ivory broadcloth
   - ivory floral print

3. Cut one 1¾" x 16" strip from each of the
   following fabrics:
   - fuchsia print
   - ivory patterned print

4. Sew aqua or yellow/lime triangles to coral
   swirl and coral burst triangles along the long
   diagonal edge. See **Overlapping & Entwined
   Triangles: Folded Over** on page 23. Follow
   Steps 1–4. Trim assembled piece so it is
   square. Place assembled piece(s) to be
   trimmed on cutting mat. Using grid-lined
   ruler, rotary cutter, and cutting mat grid,
   trim edges slightly so piece is square and
   edges are straight.

5. Sew two 23" strips together along long edge.
   Cut strip into four 5½" lengths. Sew two
   lengths to top and bottom of center section.

6. Sew two 16" strips together along long edge.
   Cut strip into eight 1¾" lengths. Sew sets of
   two cuts together in a checkerboard style,
   making four 4-patch pieces. Note: 4-patch is
   four equally sized squares sewn together to
   form a large square. Sew one 4-patch to
   either side of two remaining 5½" pieces from
   Step 5 at left. Sew to sides of center section.

7. Repeat Steps 1–6 at left and above twelve
   times for a total of thirteen blocks.

## CREATING BLOCK 2

Folding technique: Overlapping & Entwined
    Triangles: Folded-over Offset

Finished size: 10" square

Note: Enlarge pattern 200% unless otherwise
indicated.

1. Using **Triangle B** pattern on page 27, cut four
   triangles from each of the following fabrics:
   - coral burst
   - dark pink plaid
   - pink plaid

2. Cut four 1½" x 3" pieces from the coral
   burst fabric.

3. Cut one 5½" square from each of the following fabrics:
   - coral/yellow floral
   - curry solid

- terra-cotta/gold variegated
- terra-cotta plaid

4. See **Overlapping & Entwined Triangles: Folded-over Offset** on page 24. Follow Steps 1–6. Trim assembled piece so it is square. Sew coral burst triangles to each side of the center section as shown in Steps 7–8 on page 24.

5. Sew dark pink and pink plaid triangles together along shorter edges. Sew to each side of new completed center section.

6. Repeat Steps 1–5 on page 20 and above four times for a total of five blocks.

## CREATING BLOCK 3

Folding technique: Using Water Bomb Base to Create a 4-point Star Shape

Finished size: 10" square

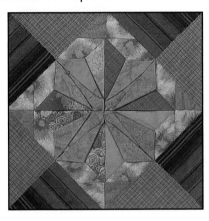

Note: Enlarge pattern 200% unless otherwise indicated.

1. Using **Triangle B** pattern on page 27, cut four triangles from each of the following fabrics:
   - dark pink plaid
   - pink plaid

2. Using **Wedge C** pattern on page 27, cut four wedges from coral burst fabric.

3. Using **Triangle D** pattern on page 27, cut four triangles from coral burst fabric.

4. Cut 3" x 5½" pieces from each of the following fabrics:

- four from pink variegated
- one from coral/yellow floral
- one from curry solid
- one from terra-cotta/gold variegated
- one from terra-cotta plaid

5. Cut four 5½" squares from curry solid fabric.

6. Using **Triangle D** pattern, cut four triangles from terra-cotta textured fabric.

7. See **Using Water Bomb Base to Create a 4-point Star Shape** on pages 25–26. Follow Steps 1–9.

8. Following Steps 10–11 on page 26, sew Wedge C pieces to four sides of center section.

9. Sew coral burst and terra-cotta textured triangles together along shorter edges. Sew triangle sets to corners of center section. Sew dark pink and pink plaid triangles together along shorter edges. Sew to each side of new center section.

10. Finish, following Step 12 on page 26.

11. Repeat Steps 1–10 at left and above six times for a total of seven blocks.

## CREATING BLOCK 4

Folding technique: Folded Triangles at Corners

Finished size: 5" square

1. Cut 5½" base squares from each of the following fabrics:
   - four from terra-cotta plaid
   - twenty from curry solid
   - twenty from ivory solid

21

2. Cut 3" squares from each of the following fabrics:
   - fifty-two from curry solid
   - sixteen from fuchsia print
   - thirty-six from ivory solid
   - twenty from terra-cotta plaid
   - twenty-eight from ivory floral
   - twenty-four from terra-cotta/gold variegated

3. See **Folded Triangles at Corners** on page 23. Follow Steps 1–2.

4. Repeat Steps 3 above forty-three times for a total of forty-four blocks.

## MAKING THE QUILT

Finished size: 60" square

1. Sew Blocks 1, 2, and 3 together in horizontal rows. Stitch horizontal rows together, forming quilt. See **Assembled Quilt Diagram** below.

| 4 is the entire border | | | | | |
|---|---|---|---|---|---|
| 1 | 3 | 1 | 3 | 1 | |
| 2 | 1 | 3 | 1 | 2 | |
| 1 | 2 | 1 | 2 | 1 | |
| 3 | 1 | 2 | 1 | 3 | |
| 1 | 3 | 1 | 3 | 1 | |
| | | | | | |

Assembled Quilt Diagram

2. For border, using Block 4, sew four sets of ten blocks together. Stitch one set to top and one set to bottom of quilt. Sew a terra-cotta/fuchsia block to ends of remaining two sets of ten. Sew to sides of quilt.

3. Sew large random-sized squares and rectangles together, using remaining pieces of fabric, to make a 64"-square backing.

4. Using basting spray or other preferred method, layer backing, batting, and quilt top together. Free-motion machine-quilt as desired.

5. Bind quilt edges with pale gold tone-on-tone fabric.

Back View of Geometric-fold Quilt

# FOLDING TECHNIQUE DIRECTIONS

## OVERLAPPING & ENTWINED TRIANGLES: FOLDED OVER

Note: The finished square size of the overlapped and entwined triangles will be the same as the right-angle edges of the triangle: a 4½" right-angle triangle will yield a 4½" square, with seam allowances included.

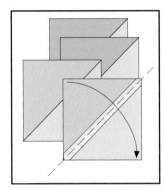 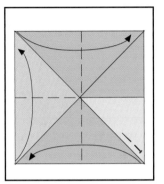 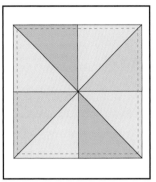 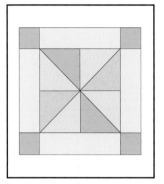

1. Press seam allowances open, then press square in half diagonally along seam line, wrong sides facing.

2. See **Overlapped & Entwinied Triangles: The Basic Technique** on page 99. Follow Steps 1–5. Fold upper-right tip of triangle down to meet lower-right corner. Pin. Rotate counterclockwise.

3. Repeat Step 2 at left with three remaining triangle tips. Press. Stitch ⅛" inward from outer edges. This is the center section of Block 1.

4. Continue with Block 1 Steps 5–6 on page 20 and sew piece into quilt block.

## FOLDED TRIANGLES AT CORNERS

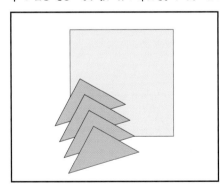 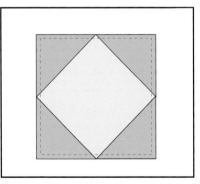

1. Fold smaller squares in half diagonally.

2. Pin and baste-stitch triangles to corners of base square, with folded edge facing center. Sew multiples of this square onto quilt as a border.

# FOLDING TECHNIQUE DIRECTIONS

## OVERLAPPING & ENTWINED TRIANGLES: FOLDED-OVER OFFSET

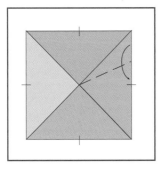 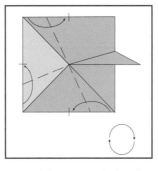 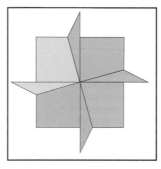 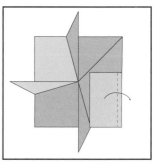

1. Press each square in half diagonally, wrong side facing. See **Overlapped and Entwined Triangles: The Basic Technique** on page 99. Follow Steps 1–5. Mark crosswise center along each outer edge.

2. Fold upper-right tip of triangle over to align with right-edge crosswise mark. Press. Rotate counterclockwise.

3. Repeat Step 2 at left for remaining sides.

4. Lift one triangular fold. Stitch narrow strip to right straight edge, beginning at inner pressed line, using ¼" seam allowance. Note: The measurement length is that from the inner pressed line to end of square.

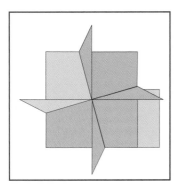 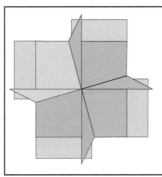 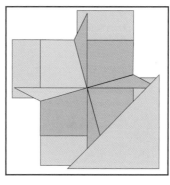 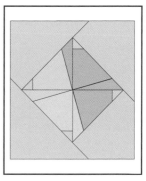

5. Press strip over. Reposition tip.

6. Repeat for remaining sides to form center section of Block 2.

7. Stitch triangle from tip of one folded-over edge to diagonal edge at next folded-over edge, using ¼" seam allowance. Press triangle open.

8. Repeat for remaining sides. Trim excess fabric under triangles. This is the completed center section for Block 2.

# FOLDING TECHNIQUE DIRECTIONS

## USING WATER BOMB BASE TO CREATE A 4-POINT STAR SHAPE

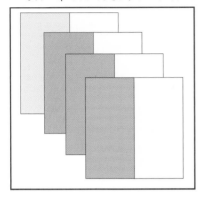

1. Sew one pink variegated rectangle to one long edge of each remaining colored rectangle. Press seam allowances open.

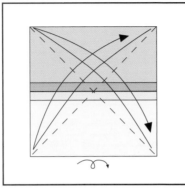

2. With fabric wrong side up, press square in half diagonally in both directions. Unfold. Notch out fabric from seam line at center. Turn piece over.

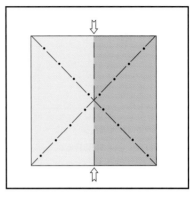

3. With fabric right side up, press square in half crosswise, thus also unpressing seam allowance. Unfold.

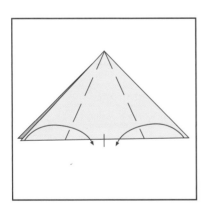

4. Collapse piece along diagonal folds, forming Water Bomb Base. Press.

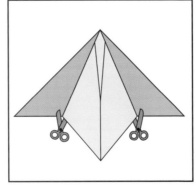

5. Bring outer tips of upper layer to center as shown. Slash fabric along new fold line on each side, ¼" inward from raw edges. Unfold piece.

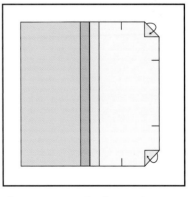

6. Measure slash marks from corners along front and sides so measurement can be referred to later. Press tips of upper-layer corners under ¼".

Continued on page 26.

Continued from page 25.

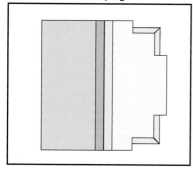

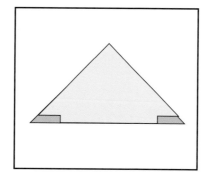

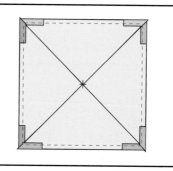

7. Press sides under ¼", at each corner to slashes forming mitered corner. Tack corner miters. Repress diagonals.

8. Refold piece as in Step 4 on page 25. Make three more Water Bomb Bases, following Steps 2–7 on page 25 and at left. Note: The measurement taken in Step 6 allows Steps 4–5 to be skipped.

9. Pin four pieces onto 5½"-square fabric piece. Tack pieces together at center and to square fabric piece. This is the center section for Block 3.

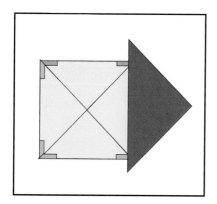

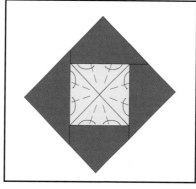

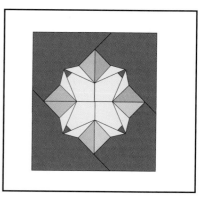

10. Sew Wedge C piece to center section: lift top layer of one Water Bomb Base piece while sewing Wedge C piece to raw edge of Water Bomb Base. Sew through to base cloth. Press seam allowance outward. Note: The Wedge C pattern is not depicted in the diagram.

11. Repeat for remaining sides.

12. Bring outer tips of each upper layer toward center and tack tips onto quilt block piece, forming a star shape.

# GEOMETRIC-FOLD QUILT PATTERNS

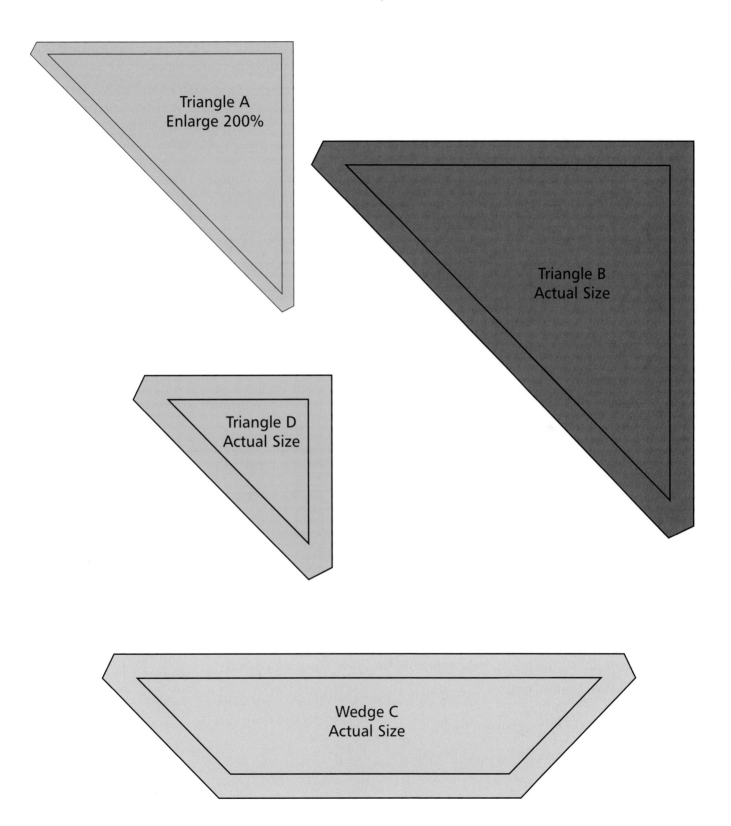

Triangle A
Enlarge 200%

Triangle B
Actual Size

Triangle D
Actual Size

Wedge C
Actual Size

# STAR WALL POCKET

## FABRICS:

Note: All fabrics are a minimum of 42" wide.

Ivory (three variations)
• Ivory textured (⅛ yd) for foundation-pieced block
• Ivory textured (½ yd) for foundation-pieced block, pocket front, pocket back, bindings
• Muslin (⅛ yd) for foundation-pieced block and star

Red (five variations)
• Ivory/red plaid (2¼" x 28") for binding
• Red broadcloth (½ yd) for star, pocket back, binding
• Red plaid (2" x 15") for pocket binding
• Red with textured appearance (¼ yd) for foundation-pieced block
• Red with white stars (¼ yd) for star

## NOTIONS:

• **Standard Tools & Notions** on page 8
• Ivory ceramic star-shaped button
• Lightweight nonwoven interfacing (½ yd)
• Matching threads

## DEFINING THE PROJECT

A 12"-square foundation-pieced block forms the upper portion of the wall pocket. This block is the backdrop for the folded-yet-traditional 8-point star.

## CREATING PIECED DESIGN BLOCK

Note: Enlarge patterns 200% unless otherwise indicated.

1. See **Foundation Piecing** on pages 15–17. Using **Foundation-piecing Patterns** on page 30, trace four of **Unit 1** and four of **Unit 2** onto nonwoven interfacing.

2. Sew fabrics onto each of the traced interfacing pieces in numerical order. Sew one Unit 1 to one Unit 2 along long diagonal edge, right sides facing. Repeat three times. Press seam allowances open. Sew four combined units together to make 12"-square foundation-pieced backdrop.

## CREATING THE STAR

Folding technique: 8-point Star

1. Cut eight 3½" x 6" pieces from red broad cloth fabric for star's outer points.

2. Cut four 3" x 6" pieces from ivory textured fabric and four from red with white stars fabric for star's inner overlapping squares. Sew each smaller piece to a larger piece along 6" edges. See **8-point Star** on page 31. Follow Steps 1–7.

3. Appliqué 8-point star to center of pieced design block (A).

## CREATING THE WALL POCKET

Finished size: 12½" x 17¼"

1. Cut one 6½" x 12½" piece from red broadcloth fabric for pocket back (B). Sew one long edge of pocket back to edge of assembled quilt block. See **Wall Pocket Diagram** at right.

2. Cut one 6½" x 12½" piece from ivory textured fabric for

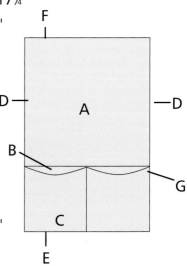

Wall Pocket Diagram

pocket front (C). Slightly scallop one long edge to indicate top of two pockets.

3. Bind scalloped edge with 2" x 15" strip of red plaid fabric (G).

4. Overlap pocket front onto back. Topstitch pocket front to back at center to form two pockets. Baste-stitch pocket front to back along side and bottom edges.

5. Cut one 12½" x 18" piece from ivory textured fabric for wall pocket back. Pin back and front together, wrong sides facing.

6. Cut two 2¼" x 18¼" strips from ivory textured fabric (D). Bind side edges.

7. Cut one 2¼" x 13½" strip from red broadcloth fabric (E). Bind bottom edge.

8. Cut one 2¼" x 28" strip from ivory/red plaid fabric (F). Fold strip in half, matching long edges. Fold in half to find center. Bind top edge, aligning center of strip with center seam of top edge.

9. Working with binding that is extending from either side of top edge, press raw edge of binding under ¼". Fold strip in half, aligning pressed-under and folded edges. Sew long edges together, turning ends under ½" when sewing.

10. Stitch button onto wall pocket.

# STAR WALL POCKET FOUNDATION-PIECING PATTERNS

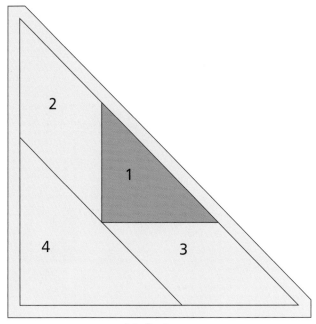

Unit 1
Enlarge 200%

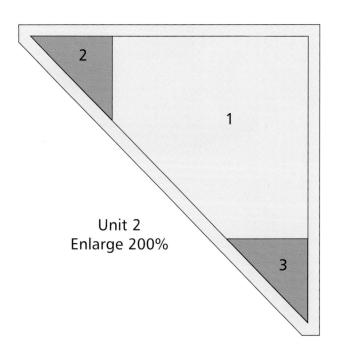

Unit 2
Enlarge 200%

30

# FOLDING TECHNIQUE DIRECTIONS

## 8-POINT STAR

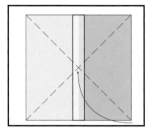

1. Press seam allowances open. Fray-preventative fabric along center edge of each side.

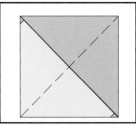

2. Press outer corners to center.

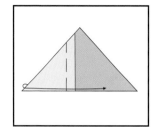

3. Press in half diagonally, positioning seam as shown.

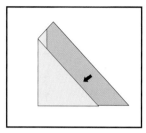

4. Fold left tip over to right, offsetting tips as shown, forming a smaller triangle as upper layer.

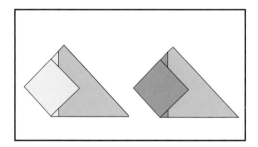

5. Lift and open right tip of upper layer, flattening layer to form a square shape. Repeat to make four from one fabric combo and four from remaining fabric combination.

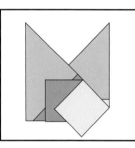

6. Lift upper layer of square and slip a contrasting folded piece within the space. Be certain star's outer points are straight along right and left edges and that center intersect forms a right angle. Pin in place on front and back sides. Repeat to overlap eight pieces.

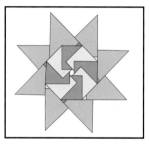

7. Stitch the pieces together from the back side and the front.

# BUTTERFLY QUILT

## FABRICS:

Note: All quilting cotton fabrics are a minimum of 42" wide.

### Floral Quilting Cotton (four variations)
- Brown floral (½ yd) for D, hearts, rod pocket binding (M)
- Three variations of pastel, dynamic-yet-soft florals (½ yd each) for butterfly, hearts, and oversized flower

### Ivory Quilting Cotton (two variations)
- Ivory tone-on-tone floral (⅓ yd) for B and hearts
- Ivory tone-on-tone patterned (⅓ yd) for D

### Periwinkle (one variation)
- 54"-wide shimmery periwinkle organza (¼ yd) for prairie points

### Soft Greens Quilting Cotton (six variations)
- Light olive green floral (½ yd) for A and backing
- Light grass tone-on-tone (½ yd) for J and stems
- Olive/orange striped (¼ yd) for butterflies and stems
- Pastel olive green patterned (½ yd) for E and backing
- Two variations of light olive geometric (½ yd each) for A and backing

### Soft Orange Quilting Cotton (one variation)
- Pastel orange speckled (½ yd) for bottom binding, oversized flower, and backing

### Soft Purples Quilting Cotton (five variations)
- Blue/lavender print (½ yd) for outer border (K), and hearts
- Dark plum (¼ yd) for butterflies

- Lavender geometric (⅓ yd) for D
- Lavender swirl (⅓ yd) for A and B
- Plum speckled (⅓ yd) for side bindings (L), and butterfly wings

### Variegated Pastel Quilting Cotton (two variations)
- Predominantly green/blue (½ yd) for G and I
- Predominantly lavender-blue (½ yd) for H, knife pleats, and butterflies

## NOTIONS:

- **Standard Tools & Notions** on page 8
- ⅛"-wide narrow cord (2 yds)
- 1"-wide olive green silk satin ribbon (2 yds)
- 1½" dia. cover button
- Beads:
  11/0 mauve seed beads
  4mm crystal iridescent, firepolish round (14)
  5mm light blue iridescent tulip-shaped (36)
  6mm crystal iridescent, flat flower-shaped (5)
  10mm aqua cloisonné (9)
  12mm crystal iridescent paillettes (11)
  short crystal bugle beads (20–30)
- Cotton batting (½ yd)
- Fusible interfacing, lightweight (¾ yd)
- Lavender iridescent machine embroidery thread
- Quilt basting spray

## DEFINING THE PROJECT

The Butterfly Quilt has a pieced backdrop that is created with subtle fabrics and some texturing. The backdrop is a random grouping of different sized squares and rectangles. The folded elements can take center stage over this pieced backdrop in an eclectic manner.

33

## CREATING THE QUILTED BACKDROP

Finished size: 35½" x 44½"

Note: All seam allowances are ¼" unless otherwise indicated.

1. Cut fabrics for backdrop, borders, and bindings as follows:

   • one 6½" square from each of two light olive geometric, one 6½" square lavender swirl, two 6½" squares from light olive floral (A)

   • one 10" square from lavender swirl, two 10" squares from ivory tone-on-tone floral

   • one 12½" x 19½" piece from lavender-blue pastel to be knife pleated (C)

   • one 10½" square from brown floral, one 10½" square from lavender geometric, and one 10½" square from ivory patterned for (D)

   • one 4½" x 10½" rectangle from pastel olive patterned for backdrop (E)

   • six 4" squares from floral fabric for half-circles (F)

   • one 2½" x 10½" strip from blue/green pastel variegated for backdrop (G)

   • one 2½" x 12½" strip from lavender-blue pastel variegated for backdrop (H)

   • two 4½" x 36" pieces from blue/green pastel variegated for inner border (I)

   • one 9" x 32½" piece from light grass tone-on-tone fabric for bottom curved border (J)

   • two 2¼" x 41" strips from blue-lavender print for outer borders (K)

   • two 2" x 41" strips from plum speckled for side binding (L)

   • one 8" x 34" piece from brown floral for rod-pocket binding (M)

   • one 6½" x 48" piece from periwinkle organza for continuous prairie points (N)

   • one 2" x 39" strip from orange speckled for bottom binding (O)

2. Cut five 8" x 44" strips from each of the following fabrics for backing:

   • one each from light olive geometrics

   • one from light olive floral

   • one from orange speckled

   • one from pastel olive

## MAKING THE PIN-TUCKED SPACES

1. Draw lines diagonally for pin-tucked squares (B), spacing lines 1⅜" apart. Fold and press fabric on each line. Stitch ⅛" from folded edge of each line to pin-tuck entire fabric square. Press pin tucks flat in one direction. With pin tucks positioned diagonally, trim pieces so each is 6½" square. After the backdrop has been created, fold a spot backward on each tuck, then tack in place.

## MAKING THE KNIFE-PLEATED SPACES

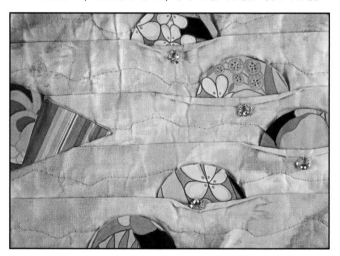

1. Beginning 2¼" from one short edge for knife pleats (C), draw lines horizontally on fabric, spacing lines 1¾" apart. Fold and press fabric on each line, then fold pressed edge into ½"-deep pleat. Pin, then baste-stitch pleats at outer edges.

2. Place two pieces (F) with right sides facing. Trace the 2¾" circle onto layered squares. Sew along traced line. Trim the excess fabric from seam allowance, leaving ⅛". Cut the

circle in half and turn each half right side out. Press. Repeat two times for a total of five-half circles.

3. At varying spaces, slip cut edges of half-circles into pleated spaces. Lift fabric to reveal underside of pleat and sew half-circles in place within the pleat. After backdrop has been created, at each half-circle location, fold pleat down ¼" and tack in place.

## PIECING THE BACKDROP

1. Working with pieces A–H, piece backdrop together. See **Butterfly Quilt Diagram** below. Work in horizontal rows to sew smaller backdrop pieces together, then to larger pieces. Sew horizontal rows together to form the backdrop.

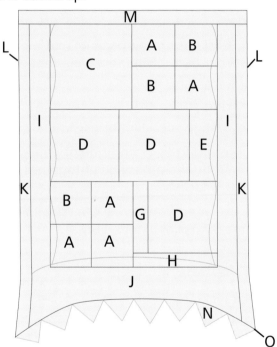

Butterfly Quilt Diagram

2. Trim sides so they have a curvy shape, cutting a bit into pieced side edges, as indicated by dotted lines on the diagram above. For side borders (I), sew a straight edge of each side border to the curvy sides. Press seam allowance toward side borders, steaming border well so that it lays flat.

3. Determine slight curve for bottom edge of quilt. Trim bottom curved edge. Use trimmed-away piece to cut bottom curved border for quilt (J). Sew curved bottom border to bottom of quilt. Press seam allowance toward border.

4. Trim inner border side edges straight, then angle outward about 1" toward bottom edges of bottom border. Sew side borders (K) to quilt sides.

## CREATING THE STEMS

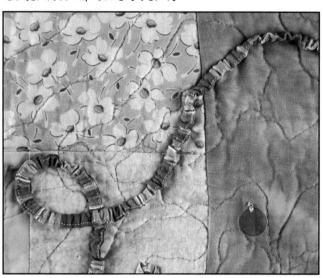

1. Cut 1¼" x 44" strips from each of the following fabrics for swirling stems:
   • one from olive/orange stripe
   • two from light grass tone-on-tone

2. See **Folded Gathered Stem** on page 44. Follow Steps 1–3. Repeat two times for a total of three stems.

3. See **Appliqué Placement Diagram** on page 38. Position and pin stems onto quilt front, swirling stems as indicated on diagram and so that one end from each length can be sewn into binding.

4. Tack tucks and pleats as noted in Step 1, **Making Pin-tucked Spaces** on page 34 and in Step 3, **Making the Knife-pleated Space** on page 34.

## ASSEMBLING THE QUILT

1. Sew five 8" x 44" assorted strips together for quilt backing, wrong side up. Place backing on work surface, wrong side up. Using quilt basting spray or other preferred method, layer backing, batting, and quilt top together. Free-motion machine-quilt as desired with lavender iridescent machine-embroidery thread.

2. Bind the side edges (L) with plum speckled fabric strips.

3. Cut six 12" lengths from ribbon. Pin one end of each ribbon length to front and back of quilt top edge at ends and center.

4. Fold brown floral rod-pocket binding (M) in half lengthwise, right sides facing. Sew short ends, turn piece right side out and press. Sew raw edge of rod-pocket binding to front of quilt-top edge, catching ribbon in while sewing. Press seam allowance toward rod-pocket binding. Fold pocket over to back and onto seam. Sew in place. Note: When hanging the quilt, tie ribbons into bows around the rod used to hang the quilt.

5. See **Continuous Prairie Points** on page 63. Note: The points are along one fabric side only. For Prairie-pointed bottom edge, cut organza strip (N) into eight 6" intervals, slicing fabric to within ½" from opposite long edge. With fabric wrong side up, press each interval in half, forming triangles. Press each triangle in half in opposite direction, forming smaller triangles.

6. Pin raw edges of continuous prairie points to bottom edge of quilt, right sides facing. Baste-stitch in place.

7. Bind bottom edge of quilt (O) with pastel orange speckled strip.

## CREATING THE OVERSIZED FLOWER

Note: Enlarge all patterns 200% unless otherwise indicated.

1. Using **Petal** pattern on page 44, cut nine petals from each of the following fabrics:
   • floral for petal front
   • interfacing
   • pastel orange speckled for each petal back

2. Fuse interfacing to wrong side of petal back. Place a front and a back petal together with right sides facing.

3. Make oversized flower. See **Oversized Flower** on page 39. Follow Steps 1–4.

## CREATING THE HEARTS

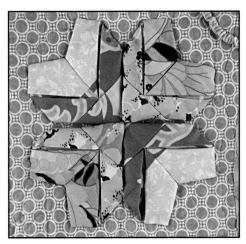

1. Cut two 3¾" x 8" pieces from blue-lavender fabric and two 7¼" x 8" from one floral fabric for two large folded hearts.

2. Cut one 3¼" x 7" piece from blue-lavender fabric and one 6½" x 7" from one floral fabric for medium folded heart.

3. Cut one 2¾" x 6" piece from blue-lavender fabric and one 5½" x 6" piece from floral fabric for small folded heart.

4. Cut two 3¾" x 8" pieces from brown floral fabric and two 7¼" x 8" pieces from one ivory tone-on-tone floral fabric for two large folded hearts.

5. See **Folded Heart** on pages 39–40. Follow, Steps 1–9. Repeat five times for a total of six hearts.

## CREATING THE BUTTERFLIES 1

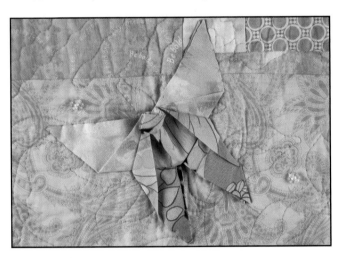

1. Cut two 5¾" x 9" pieces from one floral fabric and two 3¾" x 9" pieces from lavender-blue variegated pastel fabric for two Butterflies 1.

2. Seam one larger rectangle to one smaller rectangle. Repeat for remaining pieces. See **Folded Butterfly 1** on page 41. Follow Steps 1–7. Repeat once for a total of two Butterflies 1.

## CREATING THE BUTTERFLIES 2

1. Cut three 5¾" x 9" pieces from one floral fabric and three 3¾" x 9" pieces from dark plum fabric for three Butterflies 2.

2. Seam one larger rectangle to one smaller rectangle. Repeat for remaining pieces. See **Folded Butterfly 2** on page 42. Follow Steps 1–6. Repeat two times for a total of three Butterflies 2.

## CREATING THE BUTTERFLIES 3

1. Cut three 4¾" x 9" pieces from floral fabric for center. Cut six 2⅝" x 9" side pieces from lavender-blue variegated pastel for three Butterflies 3.

2. Seam two side pieces to one center piece. Press corners under toward wrong side, then press all edges under ¼". Repeat for remain-

ing pieces. See **Folded Butterfly 3** on page 43. Follow Steps 1–8. Repeat for two times for a total of three Butterflies 3.

## APPLIQUÉING THE ELEMENTS

1. Pin oversized the flower, the hearts, and the butterflies in place. See **Appliqué Placement Diagram** below.

Appliqué Placement Diagram

2. Stitch folded edge of stems to the quilt, leaving stitched edge free.
3. Appliqué elements to quilt front, leaving some portions of each element unattached in order to visually grasp movement within the folds.

## BEADING THE QUILT

1. Randomly stitch paillettes in place, using seed beads to anchor each one.
2. Stitch flower beads to bottom border.

3. Stitch short bugles to pin-tucks that have been tacked down.
4. Stitch bead dangles near half-circles at tacked-down knife pleats. Refer to **Bead Dangles** on page 14.
5. Using tulip-shaped bead, cloisonné bead, fire-polish bead, and seed bead as bottom bead, create nine bead dangles.
6. Stitch bead dangle in-between each prairie point and at bottom edge.

### TIP:

Cutting fabric pieces is something you may wish to do as you are ready to work with that portion of the quilt. It's easier to make some fabric decisions as the quilt progresses. Begin with the spaces in which the additional texture is added through knife pleats or pin-tucks.

# FOLDING TECHNIQUE DIRECTIONS

## OVERSIZED FLOWER

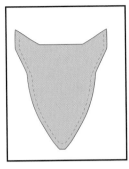

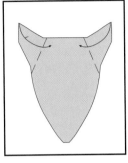

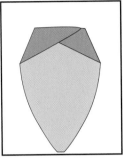

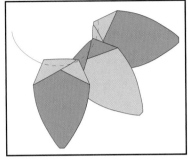

1. Sew, using ¼" seam allowance. Clip bulk from tip and edge-press.

2. Turn petal right side out, press.

3. Fold outer raw edges of petal to overlap at center, pin in place.

4. Overlap petals, alternating fronts and backs, if desired. Chain gather-stitch together, overlapping and joining last petal to first petal. Pull gathers tightly and secure thread.

## FOLDED HEART

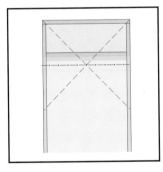

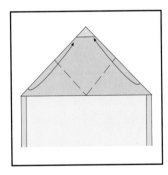

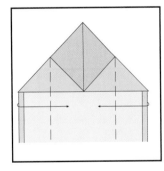

1. Cut and sew two fabric pieces to make heart. Press seam allowance open. Press under two long and one short edges ¼" toward wrong side. Note: The short edge is the one with smaller contrasting fabric piece.

2. Fold portion with seam as shown in the **Water Bomb Base** Steps 3–4 on page 25.

3. Lift left and right corners upward to meet at center top. Press.

Continued on page 40.

Continued from page 39.

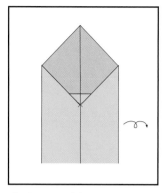

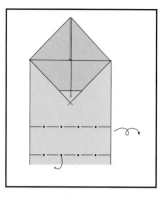

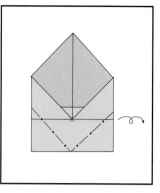

4. Press sides to center. Tack in place.

5. Turn piece over. Fold upper tip down, press, and tack.

6. Turn the piece over. Fold the lower edge up ¼", then up again to meet the point shown. Tack.

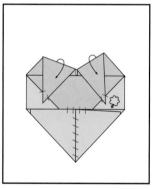

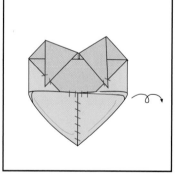

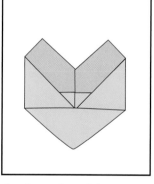

7. Press bottom edge flat. Turn the piece over. Fold bottom left and right corners diagonally up. Tack in place. Fold upper points diagonally down and tack, forming heart shape.

8. Lightly stuff the little pocket on lower half of heart with batting.

9. Completed heart.

# FOLDING TECHNIQUE DIRECTIONS

## FOLDED BUTTERFLY 1

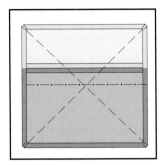

1. Press seam allowance open. Press corners under to wrong side, then press all edges under ¼".

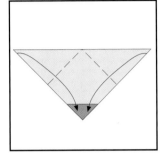

2. Fold piece into **Water Bomb Base**, following Steps 3–4 on page 25.

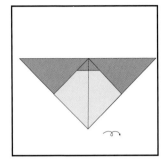

3. Fold top layer of right- and left-upper tips down to lower-center tip, press.

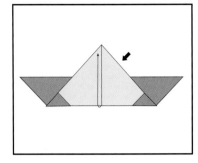

4. Turn the piece over. Fold the bottom upward, press.

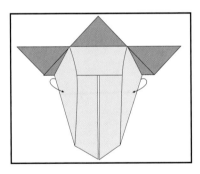

5. Lift upper-center tips and extend them down fully. The sides will automatically fold inward slightly. Press.

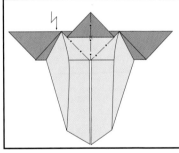

6. Make stair-step fold with upper tip. Tack.

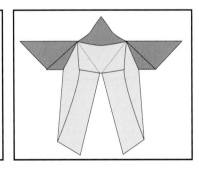

7. Fold form in half and pinch center, then open and flatten wings. This will cause the body to form diagonally to lower wing. Tack body.

# FOLDING TECHNIQUE DIRECTIONS

## FOLDED BUTTERFLY 2

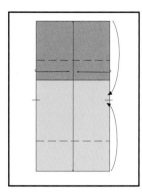

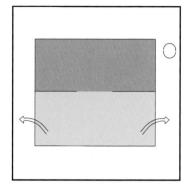

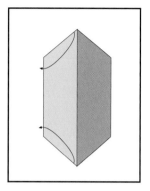

1. With seamed position as shown, press piece in half, then press sides to center.

2. Press top and bottom edges to center.

3. Rotate piece to right. Pull inner-center corners outward, press. The larger fabric piece should be positioned on left side.

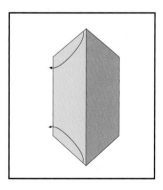

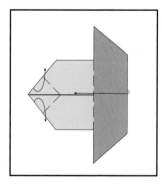

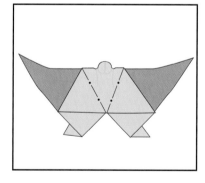

4. Fold left side top and bottom tips to left.

5. Fold left tips diagonally. Fold right side onto left side.

6. Turn piece over. Fold in half and fold center diagonally to form body. Push top inward and tack to hold body in place.

# FOLDING TECHNIQUE DIRECTIONS

## FOLDED BUTTERFLY 3

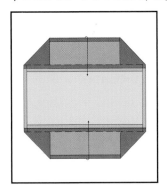

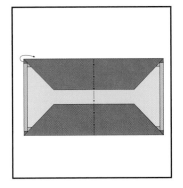

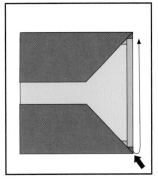

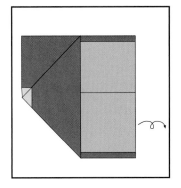

1. With fabric wrong side up, press the corners over as shown.

2. Press top and bottom edges over along edge of corner folds.

3. Press in half, right sides facing.

4. Lift lower-right corner upward. Flatten space to from a triangle.

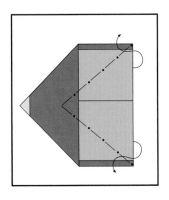

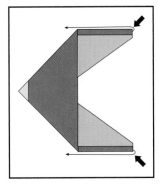

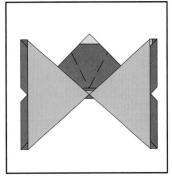

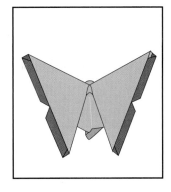

5. Turn piece over and repeat Step 4 above.

6. Lift upper layer of upper-right corner and make an insider reverse fold. Repeat with lower-right corner.

7. Lift right sides, open and flatten, forming two larger triangles at top and bottom.

8. Fold in half and fold center diagonally to form body. Tack center of body for more texture.

# FOLDING TECHNIQUE DIRECTIONS

## FOLDED GATHERED STEM

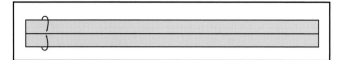

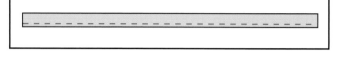

1. Press long edges inward to center.

2. Press in half again and sew edges together, forming a tube.

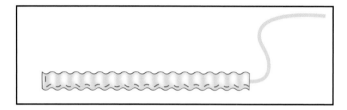

3. Thread narrow cord through tube. Secure cord to one end, then pull on cord from other end to gather tube. Repeat Steps 1–3 above for remaining pieces.

# BUTTERFLY QUILT PATTERN

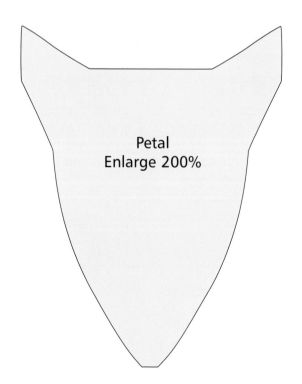

Petal
Enlarge 200%

# ROSES QUILT

# ROSES QUILT

## FABRICS:

Note: All fabrics are a minimum of 42" wide.

### Ecru (seven variations)
- Ecru washable wool (⅞ yd) for quilt back ground
- Four dark variations of ecru quilting cotton (¼ yd each) for outer edge swirls
- Two light variations of ecru quilting cotton (¼ yd each) for outer edge swirls

### Gold Quilting Cotton (three variations)
- Gold patterned (1 yd) for backing
- Light brownish gold (¼ yd) for binding
- Very pale gold (½ yd) for vase and bias edge for swirls

### Gray Quilting Cotton (one variation)
- Gray (¼ yd) for bust and vase outlines

### Green Quilting Cotton (nine variations)
- Five variations of light green (⅛ yd each) for leaves
- Pale olive green (¼ yd) for leaves
- Three variations of dark green (⅛ yd each) for leaves

### Ivory Quilting Cotton (nine variations)
- Ivory (⅓ yd) for overall body shape
- Five variations of ivory (one 6" sq. each) for face
- Three variations of ivory (¼ yd each) for clothing

### Neutral-colored Quilting Cotton (five variations)
- Assorted neutrals (4" x 8" each) for lettering

### Pink Quilting Cotton (ten variations)
- Five variations of medium (6" x 8" each) for flowers
- Three muted variations of light pink (⅛ yd of each) for flowers Note: Consider using the back side of certain fabrics for greater subtlety.
- Two very muted variations of light pink (¼ yd of each) for flowers

## NOTIONS:
- **Fabric Printing Tools** on page 9
- **Standard Tools & Notions** on page 8
- Cotton batting (½ yard)
- Craft scissors
- Fabric glue
- Loop turner
- Machine-embroidery threads:
  dark green
  light green
- Pinking shears
- Poster board (20" x 30" sheet)
- Quilt basting spray
- Quilting threads:
  ecru
  ivory
  rose
- Transparent tape

## DEFINING THE PROJECT

The Roses Quilt shown on page 45 is a study in subtlety. It has been purposely presented almost entirely in neutrals. One clearly sees that there is a vase filled with lovely roses in the midst of many leaves. One clearly sees that Roses has been spelled out in large letters. But one has to study the quilt for an occasion to read about a life or portions of a poem and an opportunity to speak from within.

## MAKING THE QUILT

Finished size: 26¼" x 31¼"

Note: Enlarge patterns 200% unless otherwise indicated.

1. Enlarge **Bust** pattern on page 55, **Flower** patterns on pages 53–54, **Leaf** patterns on page 59, **Roses Lettering** pattern on page 59, **Swirl** patterns on pages 56–58, and **Vase** patterns on page 54.

2. Use tracing paper to make overlay patterns for bust. Position paper onto full-sized bust piece that has been enlarged. The elements for bust are numbered. They are applied to the overall shape in numerical order and certain portions of a sequential element are overlapped onto another. For instance, piece 1 is the full-sized bust. The other pieces are overlaid onto it, except at forehead, neck, and arm.

3. Place piece 2 next, but notice that pieces 3 and 8 overlap onto some of 2. Where those pieces overlap, add ¼" underlap allowance to 2 when making pattern from tracing paper. Pieces 4 and 8 overlap onto some of 3. Where those pieces overlap, add ¼" underlap allowance to 3 pattern. Piece 10 overlaps onto 9 and 11. Where 10 overlaps onto them, add ¼" underlap allowance to 9 and 11 patterns.

4. Once the bust overlay patterns have been traced onto the paper, tape each pattern to poster board. Cut out patterns from poster board, making sturdy patterns. Be certain to label each pattern. If preferred, make sturdy patterns for the flowers, leaves, and lettering from poster board in the same manner.

5. Once a pattern has been traced onto the back side of fabric and prior to cutting piece out, lightly spray starch onto fabric. Note: This will keep the fabric from fraying both before and after it has been stitched in place. The use of spray starch does away with the need to use a fusible adhesive, thus eliminating the stiffness caused by a fusible adhesive.

6. Preshrink washable wool. Preshrink cotton batting by misting it with water-filled spray bottle, then ironing dry.

7. Assemble quilt by creating the individual elements. See **Roses Quilt Diagram** below.

Roses Quilt Diagram

## CREATING THE ELEMENTS

1. Cut 29" x 43" piece from wool fabric. Using pencil and a light source, transfer placement of vase, flowers, bust, and roses lettering onto wool, including rose at bottom-left corner of quilt.

2. Cut 31" x 44" piece from gold patterned fabric for backing. Set aside for now. Cut two 1½" x 32½" strips and two 1½" x 27½" strips from light golden brown fabric for outer edge binding.

3. Assemble bust, vase, roses lettering, and flowers onto cotton batting individually. Apply bust, vase, rose lettering, leaves, and flowers to wool background piece in that order, keeping in mind the manner in which the elements play off each other.

## CREATING THE BUST

1. Using **Bust** pattern, trace and cut bust from ivory fabric. Using left side edge of bust pattern (this will be a shadow), trace and cut 1"-wide piece from gray fabric for binding.

2. Using poster board patterns from Step 2 on page 47, trace and cut individual face and clothing elements from ivory variations for bust.

3. Cut a piece of cotton batting 1" larger all around than vase. Pin journaled vase to batting. See **Journaling on the Fabric**, Steps 1–3 at right. Machine-quilt the two layers together. Very lightly adhere face and clothing elements onto bust, working with one element at a time in numerical order. Machine-buttonhole-stitch elements to bust. Trim batting away from bust.

4. Pin bust shadow in place on wool. When comfortable with the anticipated surrounding elements, machine-buttonhole-stitch shadow onto wool. Pin quilted bust in place on wool so it is slightly offset of the shadow. Machine-buttonhole-stitch bust onto wool.

## CREATING THE VASE

1. Using **Vase** and **Vase Side** patterns, trace and cut from pale gold fabric. Set vase side aside for now.

2. Using left side edge of **Vase** pattern (this will be a shadow), trace and cut a 1"-wide piece from gray fabric.

3. Cut piece of cotton batting 1" larger all around than vase. Pin journaled vase to batting and machine-quilt the two pieces together horizontally in-between each line of prose. Trim batting away from vase.

4. Pin vase shadow in place on wool, overlapping onto right side of bust. Machine button-hole-stitch shadow to wool. Trim away excess bust. Pin quilted vase in place on wool so it is slightly offset of the shadow. Machine-buttonhole-stitch vase to wool.

5. Cut a piece of cotton batting 1" larger all around than vase Side. Pin vase side to batting. Machine buttonhole-stitch vase side to batting. Trim batting away from vase side. Note: The vase side does not have a shadow.

6. Machine-buttonhole-stitch vase side to wool.

## JOURNALING ON THE FABRIC

1. To transfer a letter, poem, or prose of choice to fabric, begin by reading the ink-jet transfer paper manufacturer's instructions.

   Option #1:
   Photocopy your letter, poem, or prose onto transfer paper at your local copy shop so that the lettering is backward.

**Option #2:**

Working with a computer in an image-editing program in a new file, such as for making a sign, choose a text box. Enlarge text box to full size. Using font types and sizes desired, type phrase, etc. in the text box. Select "Flip" in the Effects drop-down menu. Select "Flip Horizontally." This will reverse lettering, so that it is backwards. Print phrase onto non-grid side of transfer paper. To cover entire Vase with lettering will require 1¼ sheets of printed prose.

2. Place press cloth over hard pressing surface. Heat iron (do not use steam). Place fabric Vase right side up over press cloth. Trim phrase from transfer paper with the deckle-edged scissors so there is a scant ⅛" border all around.

3. Cut paper into two pieces between two lines of prose. Note: It is easier to work with a smaller piece when transferring the lettering onto the fabric. Place transfer paper image face down in place on fabric. Apply hot dry iron with heavy pressure to paper for approximately 45 seconds, moving iron in a slow circular motion so whole image is pressed firmly for same length of time. Allow fabric to cool for a second, then peel away backing paper in one smooth movement. Do not iron directly on transferred image. To remove shiny appearance on fabric from image transfer, iron over image, using the silicone press sheet. Continue to apply your image to entire fabric vase piece.

## CREATING THE ROSES LETTERING

1. Using **Roses Lettering** pattern, trace and cut lettering from five variations of neutral fabrics. Pin, then very lightly glue lettering onto cotton batting.

2. Using pinking shears, trim batting from lettering, allowing for a slight pinked-batting border around each letter.

3. Machine-buttonhole-stitch lettering in place on wool, overlapping it onto portions of the bust and vase.

## CREATING THE LEAVES

1. Using **Leaf 1–4** patterns, trace and cut four of each pattern from dark green variations of fabric.

2. Place a bed of dark green leaves on wool near vase flowers only (do not place the dark green leaves at the bottom-left corner of the quilt at this time). Pin, then very lightly adhere leaves into place. Note: The dark green leaves are used to add depth to the overall imagery.

3. Using narrow zigzag stitch and dark green machine-embroidery thread, use free-motion option on sewing machine to machine-embroider leaves in place.

4. Using **Leaf 1–5** patterns, trace and cut seven of each leaf from light green variations of fabrics. Place a bed of light green leaves over dark green leaves near vase flowers, overlapping leaves in all directions. Pin, then very lightly adhere leaves into place. Machine-embroider leaves onto backdrop. Refer to Step 3 above.

5. Cut four ⅝" x 9" strips from palest olive green fabric for bias. Fold one strip in half, matching long edges, right sides together. Stitch a scant ⅛" from raw edges. Using loop turner, turn right side out, forming a narrow stem. Repeat with remaining pieces. Pin and lightly adhere stems in place.

6. Using **Leaf 6** pattern, trace and cut 21 leaves from light green variations of fabrics. Pin,

49

then lightly adhere leaves in place on stems. Machine-embroider leaves and stems onto backdrop. Refer to Step 3 on page 49.

## CREATING THE FLOWERS

1. Using **Flowers 1, 2, 3** and **5** patterns, trace and cut the following flowers from dark pink fabric variations: three of flower 1, three of flower 2, one of flower 3, and one of flower 5.

2. Cut one piece of cotton batting 1" larger all around than each flower. Pin flowers to batting, then very lightly adhere flowers onto batting. Machine-buttonhole-stitch flowers in place onto backdrop as the bottom layer for dimensional flowers.

## CREATING THE RIBBONWORK FLOWERS

1. Cut fifteen 1¾" x 4" pieces from muted pink fabrics for Part 1. Cut fifteen 2¼" x 4" pieces from muted pink fabrics for Part 2. Cut three 2¼" circles from muted pink fabrics. Note: Each flower has five petals.

2. See **Ribbonwork Petal Flowers** on page 52. Follow Steps 1–9. Repeat twice for a total of three flowers.

## CREATING THE FOUR-PETALLED FLOWERS

1. Use **Flower 2–5** patterns, make three of flower 2, four of flower 3, three of flower 4, and one of flower 5.

2. See **Four-petalled Flowers** on page 53. Follow Steps 1–5 to make a total of eleven flowers. Note: Once the swirls have been stitched to the backdrop, the flowers will be hand-stitched in place.

## CREATING THE SWIRLS

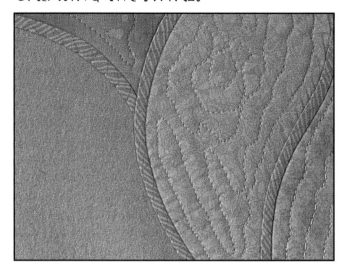

1. Using **Swirl 3** pattern and **Swirl 5** pattern, cut one each from first dark ecru fabric.

2. Using **Swirl 7** pattern, cut one from second variation of dark ecru fabric.

3. Using **Swirl 11** pattern, cut one from third variation of dark ecru fabric.

4. Using **Swirl 10** pattern, cut one from fourth dark ecru fabric.

5. Using **Swirl 1, 4,** and **9** patterns, cut one each from first light ecru fabric.

6. Using **Swirl 2, 6,** and **8** patterns, cut one of each from second light ecru fabric.

7. Cut 1"-wide bias strips from pale gold fabric for a total of 150". Sew the strips together.

8. Pin Swirl 1 in place.

9. Press 1"-wide bias strip in half lengthwise, matching long edges. Align raw edges of bias with inner edge of Swirl 1. Stitch, using ¼" seam allowance. Trim seam to ⅛". Press bias toward seam allowance. Stitch folded edge of bias to backdrop fabric, creating a finished edge for swirl.

10. Add swirls to backdrop in numerical order, so where swirl 1 meets swirl 2, swirl 2 will

overlap onto swirl 1, and so on. Finish each inner edge with bias. Refer to Step 3. Note: The swirls on the right side edge will require longer pieces of bias, as they are finished in place as if working with two long swirls.

11. Cut 1"-wide bias strip from pale olive green fabric for rose stem. Press in half, matching long edges. Stitch raw edge of bias along upper edge of swirl 10, crossing over to upper edge of swirl 8, simulating rose stem at lower-left corner of quilt.

## CREATING THE FINAL ROSE

1. Place a bed of dark green and light green leaves at lower-left corner of quilt. Free-motion stitch in place.

2. Place two pieces of green fabric with right sides facing, having back fabric on top. Using pencil, trace around Leaf 1 pattern. Stitch around traced line, leaving the top edge of leaf unsewn. Trim a scant ⅛" from stitching. Turn leaf right side out through opening. Using crochet needle, push out seam line. Press.

3. Repeat Step 2 above for as many "free" leaves as desired.

4. Position "free" leaves in place at bottom left corner of quilt where final rose will be placed so that inner edges of leaves will be underneath final rose's bottom layer. Sew upper edge of leaves onto backdrop.

5. Sew center of set-aside rose over leaves.

## FINISHING THE QUILT

1. Stitch one or two 4-petalled flowers onto each buttonhole-stitched rose. Stitch three ribbonwork flowers onto two roses in vase and rose at lower-left corner.

2. Trim quilt to 26¼" x 31¼".

3. Using basting spray or other preferred method, layer backing, and quilt top together, wrong sides facing. Free-motion machine-quilt as desired.

4. Using light brownish gold binding strips, bind quilt.

# FOLDING TECHNIQUE DIRECTIONS

## RIBBONWORK PETAL FLOWERS

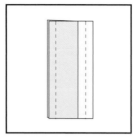

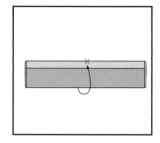

1. Sew Part 1 piece to Part 2 piece along one long edge, using ¼" seam allowance. Press seam allowance toward narrower piece.

2. Sew remaining long edges together, forming a tube. Press seam allowance toward narrow piece.

3. Turn tube right side out. Position narrow piece at center of wider piece. Press.

4. Fold tube in half, matching pressed edges. Stitch centers of long edges together.

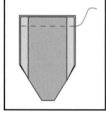

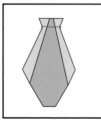

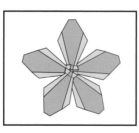

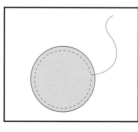

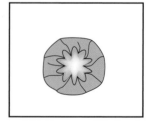

5. Open out piece and fold in half, matching raw edges. Gather-stitch through both layers ¼" from raw edges.

6. Pull gathers taut and wrap thread two times around gathers. Knot thread.

7. Repeat Steps 1–6 above and at left four times for a total of five petals. Stitch petals together along gathered edges, forming flower.

8. Using 2¼" circle, gather-stitch ⅛" from raw edge to form yo-yo center.

9. Pull gathers taut and knot thread. Turn piece over. Stitch yo-yo to center of flower.

# FOLDING TECHNIQUE DIRECTIONS

## FOUR-PETALED FLOWERS

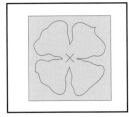  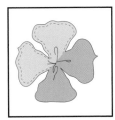 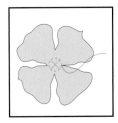 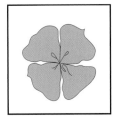

1. Place two pieces of fabric with right sides facing, having back fabric on top. Using pencil, trace around flower pattern. Slash center of top (this is back) layer only.

2. Stitch on traced line. Trim a scant 1/8" from stitching. Snip to each inner point.

3. Turn flower right side out through the slashes.

4. Using crochet needle, push out seam line. Press. Trace 3/4" circle at center of flower back side. Gather-stitch around the circle.

5. Pull stitches taut and knot thread.

# ROSES QUILT PATTERNS

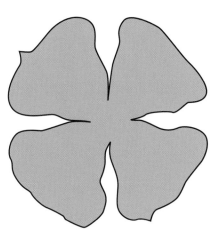

Flower 1
Enlarge 200%

Flower 2
Enlarge 200%

Flower 3
Enlarge 200%

# ROSES QUILT PATTERNS

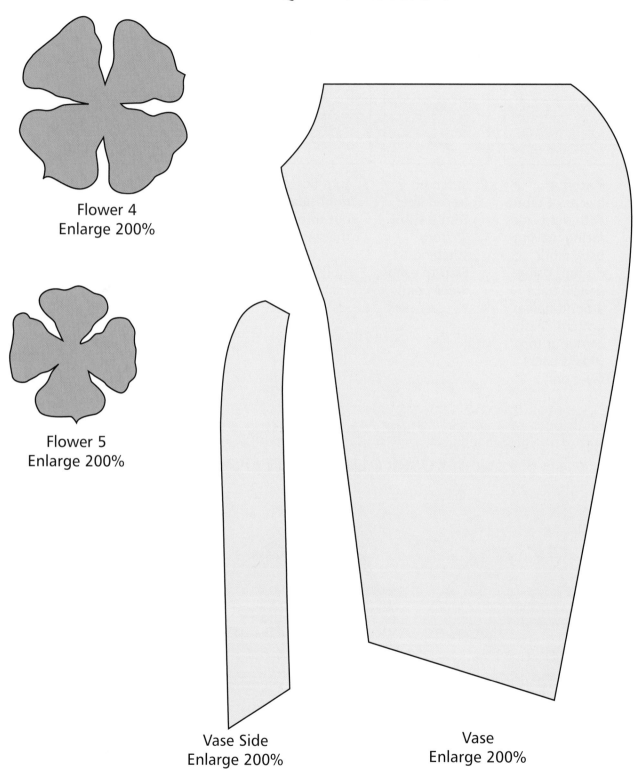

Flower 4
Enlarge 200%

Flower 5
Enlarge 200%

Vase Side
Enlarge 200%

Vase
Enlarge 200%

# ROSES QUILT PATTERNS

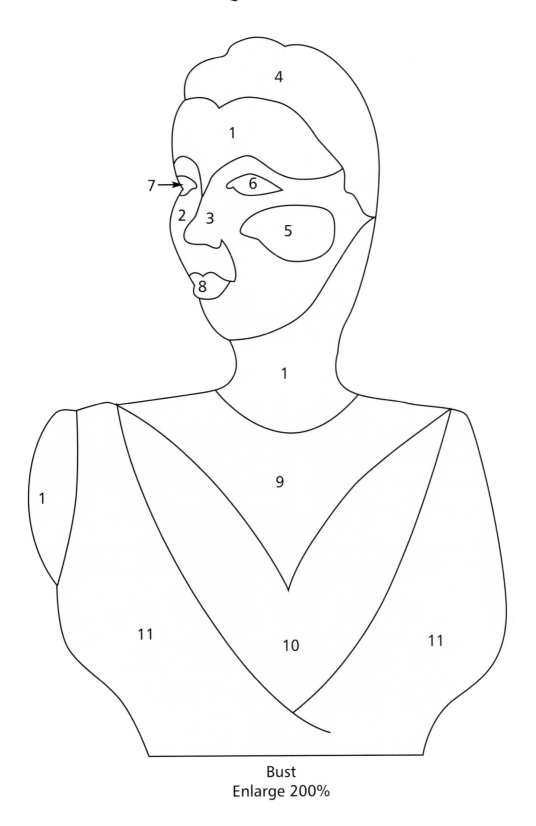

Bust
Enlarge 200%

# ROSES QUILT PATTERNS

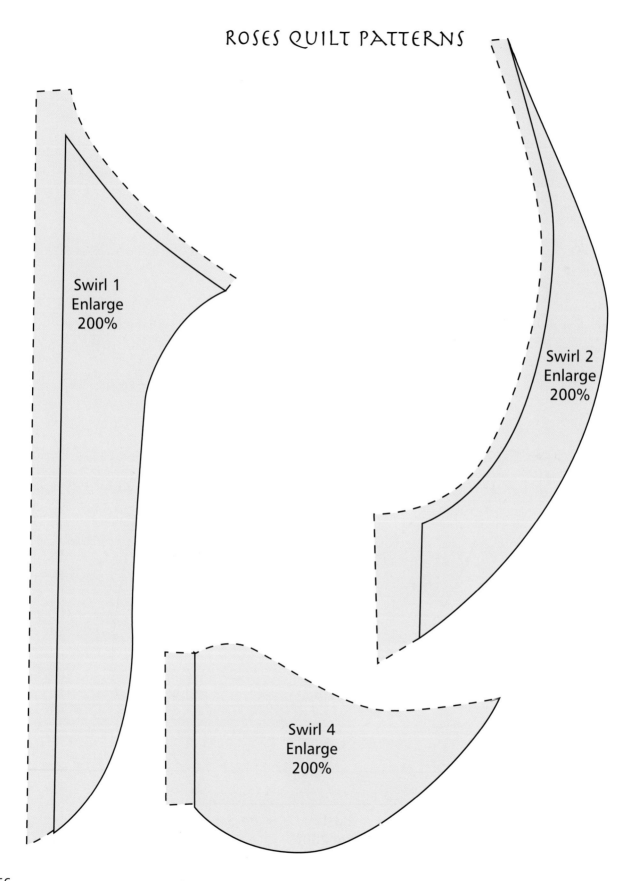

Swirl 1
Enlarge
200%

Swirl 2
Enlarge
200%

Swirl 4
Enlarge
200%

# ROSES QUILT PATTERNS

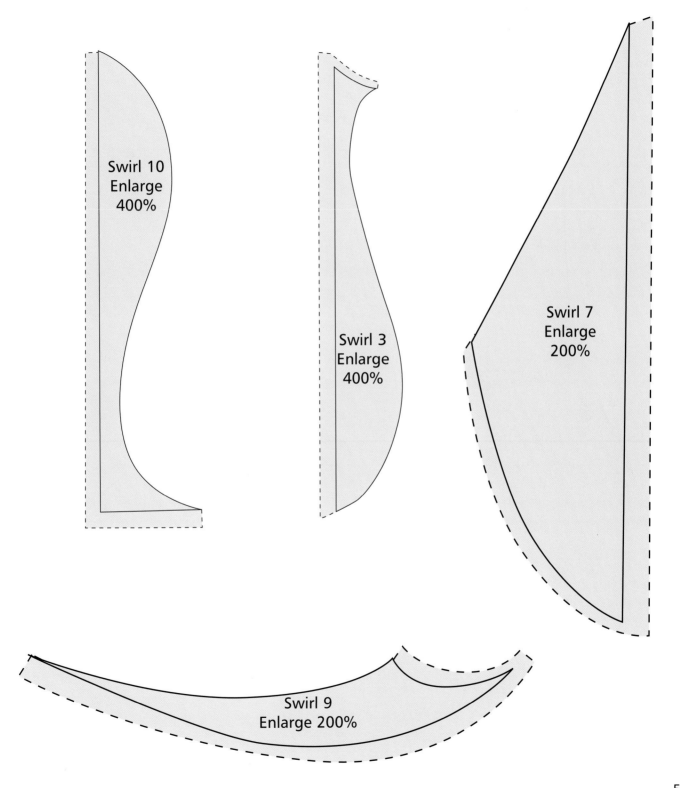

Swirl 10
Enlarge
400%

Swirl 3
Enlarge
400%

Swirl 7
Enlarge
200%

Swirl 9
Enlarge 200%

# ROSES QUILT PATTERNS

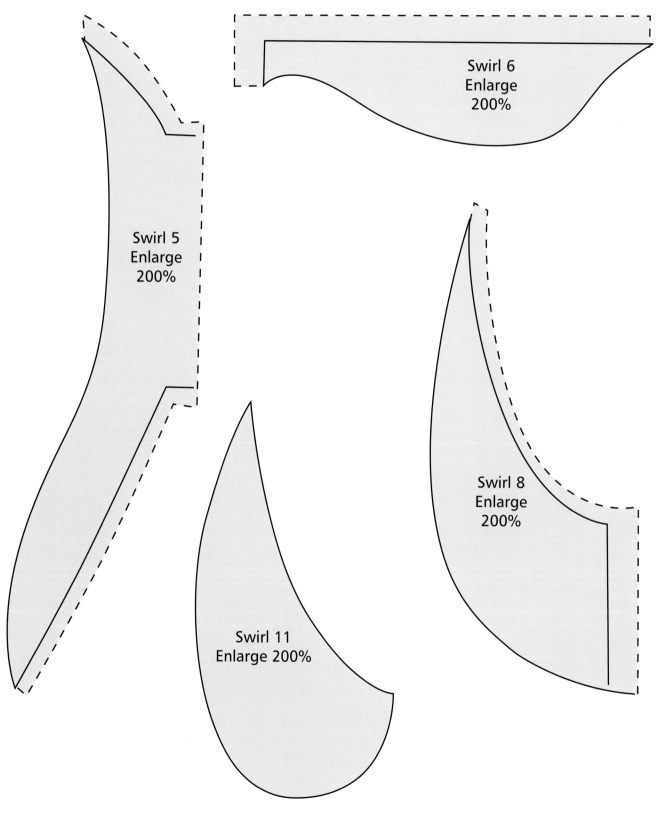

Swirl 6
Enlarge
200%

Swirl 5
Enlarge
200%

Swirl 8
Enlarge
200%

Swirl 11
Enlarge 200%

# ROSES QUILT PATTERNS

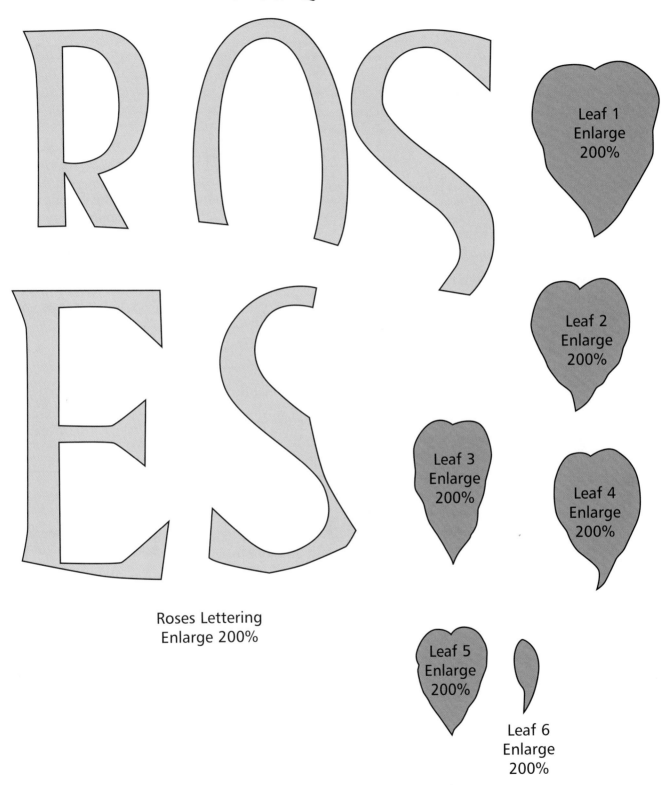

Leaf 1
Enlarge
200%

Leaf 2
Enlarge
200%

Leaf 3
Enlarge
200%

Leaf 4
Enlarge
200%

Leaf 5
Enlarge
200%

Leaf 6
Enlarge
200%

Roses Lettering
Enlarge 200%

# CELESTIAL LOTUS DESIGN

## FABRICS:

### Green (five variations)
- Three variations of green silk (⅛ yd of each) for lotus (B & C)
- Green cross-dyed dupioni (⅛ yd) for journal area (D)
- Greenish-taupe dupioni (⅛ yd) for side (F & G) and bottom bindings (I)
- Teal washable wool (10½" x 14½") for backing

### Peach (one variation)
- Peach silk organza (⅛ yd) for prairie points

### Rust (one variation)
- Rust dupioni (⅛ yd) for photo backing (A) and top binding (H)

### Tan (eight variations)
- Dark tan linen (⅛ yd) for bottom journal area (E)
- Four variations of tan silk or satin (⅛ yd each) for lotus (B & C)
- Three variations of tan velvet (⅛ yd) for lotus (B & C)

## NOTIONS:
- **Standard Notions & Tools** on page 8
- Beads:
  11/0 green seed
  4mm clear/peach firepolish (5)
  6mm brown pearl (5)
- Canvas photo fabric (8½" x 11" sheet)
- Embroidery flosses:
  light green
  olive green
  rust
- Lightweight fusible interfacing (¼ yd)
- Nonwoven interfacing (not fusible) (¼ yd)
- Permanent ink gel pens: shades close to floss colors

- Photos (2)
- Size 3 embroidery needle
- Wooden dowel or rod

## DEFINING THE PROJECT

For the sake of simplicity, the fabric list suggests a ⅛ yard requirement for most fabrics. The scrapbook pages offer an opportunity to showcase a collection of diminutive pieces of treasured fabrics, otherwise known as scraps, along with some treasured buttons and beads that may have come from Grandma's clothing and jewelry. Enjoy the collecting process as you put together our silk scrapbook page.

## CREATING THE SCRAPBOOK PAGE

1. Photocopy photos onto canvas photo fabric, following manufacturer's instructions. Crop one photograph to 2¾" circle. Crop or tear remaining photo to 3" x 6".

2. Cut fabric pieces as follows:
   - one 3¾" x 6½" piece from rust for photo backing (A)
   - one 3¾" x 10½" piece from green cross-dyed dupioni for journal area (D)
   - one 4½" x 10½" piece from dark tan linen for bottom journal area (E)
   - two 1½" x 14" strips from greenish-taupe dupioni fabric for side binding (F & G)
   - one 2½" x 10½" strip from rust silk dupioni for top binding (H)
   - one 1½" x 10½" strip from greenish-taupe dupioni for bottom binding (I)
   - one 10½" x 14½" piece from teal for backing

3. Interface fabrics that need a bit more body. Note: Some of the lighter weight fabrics will be more manageable if interfaced.

Continued on page 62.

Continued from page 60.

## CREATING THE JOURNAL AREA

1. Print words you wish to journal from a computer. Using permanent ink pen that is similar to embroidery floss, transfer lettering to right side of fabric (D & E). Heat-set ink with iron. Another option would be to transfer the journaling onto fabric, using ink-jet transfer paper. Refer to **Journaling on the Fabric** on pages 48–49. You may simply wish to handwrite your journaling with a fabric writing pen or fabric paint.

2. Backstitch journaling with three strands of embroidery floss. Note: Embroidered journaling must be done prior to piecing the page together.

## CREATING THE CELESTIAL LOTUS BLOCK

Finished size for each half: 3" x 6"

1. Refer to **Foundation Piecing** on pages 15–17. Using **Foundation-piecing Patterns** on page 64, trace two of **Unit 1** onto nonwoven interfacing, making one right and make one left. Trace two of **Unit 2** onto nonwoven interfacing, making one right and one left.

2. Make Celestial Lotus from silk, satin, and velvet fabric variations. Sew pieces to foundation in numerical order.

3. Stitch Unit 1 left to Unit 2 left for Celestial Lotus Left. Stitch Unit 1 right to Unit 2 right for Celestial Lotus Right. See **Assembled Section Diagram** at right.

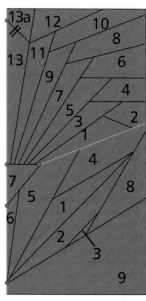

Assembled Section Diagram

## ASSEMBLING THE SCRAPBOOK PAGE

1. Sew page together in alphabetical order. See **Scrapbook Page Diagram** below. Begin by pinning 3" x 6" cropped photo to A piece. Pin and stitch circular photo to left side of D piece with decorative machine-embroidery stitch.

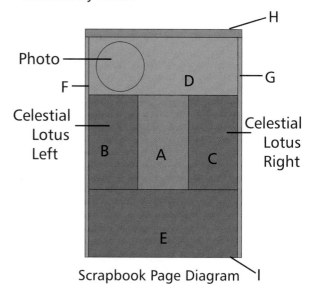

Scrapbook Page Diagram

2. Stitch assembled Celestial Lotus Left to left edge of A, leaving photo edge free. Stitch assembled Celestial Lotus Right to right edge of A in same manner. Stitch D to top and E to bottom of Celestial Lotus section.

3. Place scrapbook page on top of backing fabric, wrong sides facing. Bind side edges of page with F & G strips.

4. Fold top binding (H) in half lengthwise, right sides facing. Sew short ends, turn piece right side out and press.

5. Sew raw edge of rod- pocket binding to right side of top edge. Press seam toward rod-pocket binding. Fold binding over to back side and onto seam, Stitch in place, leaving side edges open.

6. Insert dowel or rod to hang scrapbook page.

## CREATING THE PRAIRIE POINTS

1. Cut 4¼" x 10" piece from peach fabric for prairie points

2. See **Folding Continuos Prairie Points** on below. Follow Steps 1–4.

## FINISHING THE SCRAPBOOK PAGE

1. Pin straight edge of continuos prairie points to bottom edge of scrapbook, right sides facing. Bind bottom edge with I strip. Press points downward.

2. Stitch a bead dangle onto every other prairie point. Refer to **Bead Dangles** on page 14.

# FOLDING TECHNIQUE DIRECTIONS

## FOLDING CONTINUOS PRAIRIE POINTS

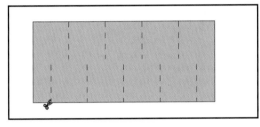

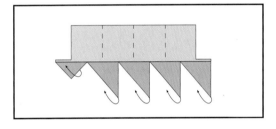

1. Press piece in half, lengthwise. Slice fabric to within ⅛" from center at 2" intervals along one side. Along remaining side, beginning 1" from end, slice fabric in the same manner in 2" intervals. The first side will have one less interval than the second side.

2. Trim away 1" piece of fabric at ends of second side. With fabric wrong side up, press each interval in half, forming triangles. Press each triangle in half in opposite direction, forming smaller triangles.

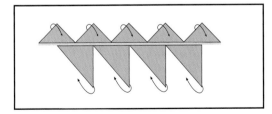

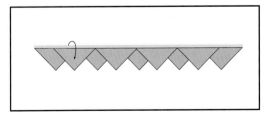

3. Working with remaining side, press each interval into smaller triangle, as in Step 2 above.

4. Fold piece in half lengthwise so that triangles from one side are centered between triangles on other side. Insert piece into a seam, taking at least a ¼" seam allowance.

# CELESTIAL LOTUS DESIGN
# FOUNDATION-PIECING PATTERNS

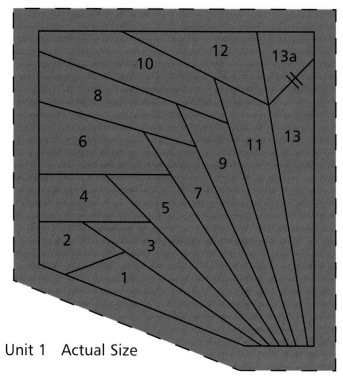

Unit 1   Actual Size

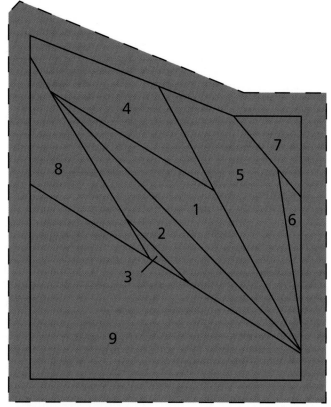

Unit 2   Actual Size

# LOTUS BLOSSOM DESIGN

## FABRICS:

### Brown (one variation)
- Dark brown silk (⅛ yd) for bottom binding (J)

### Cream (one variation)
- Cream washable wool (⅛ yd) for top journal area (F) and backing

### Gold (one variation)
- Gold taffeta (⅛ yd) for lotus (B & C)

### Green (six variations)
- Green dupioni (⅛ yd) for side (G & H) and top bindings (I)
- Four variations of green satin (⅛ yd) for lotus (B & C)
- Light green flannel (⅛ yd) for bottom section (E)

### Mauve (one variation)
- Mauve taffeta (⅛ yd) for lotus (B & C)

### Peach (one variation)
- Peach silk organza (8" x 16") for blinzes

### Rust (one variation)
- Rust silk dupioni (⅛ yd) for blinzes strip (D), lotus (B & C), and photo strip (A)

### Tan (one variation)
- Tan silk (⅛ yd) for lotus (B & C)

## NOTIONS:

- **Standard Notions & Tools** on page 8
- ½"-wide red/gold jacquard ribbon (9")
- Beads:
  11/0 green seeds (100)
  4mm clear/peach firepolish (12)
  green leaf-shaped (9)
- Canvas photo fabric (8½" x 11" sheet)
- Embroidery flosses:
  blue
  rust
- Lightweight fusible interfacing (¼ yd)
- Nonwoven interfacing (not fusible) (¼ yd)
- Permanent ink gel pens shades close to floss colors
- Photo
- Size 3 embroidery needle
- Wooden dowel or rod

## CREATING THE SCRAPBOOK PAGE

1. Photocopy photograph onto canvas photo fabric, following manufacturer's instructions for correct procedure. Crop photo to fit space A and so that it extends onto space D.

2. Cut fabric pieces as follows:
   - one 2½" x 4½" piece from rust dupioni for photo backing (A)
   - one 3⅜" x 10½" piece from rust dupioni for blinzes strip (D)
   - one 2¼" x 10½" strip from light green flannel for bottom section (E)
   - one 3⅞" x 10½" piece from cream wool for top journal area (F)
   - two 1½" x 13" strips from green dupioni fabric for side bindings (G & H)
   - one 1½" x 10" strip from green dupioni for top binding (I)
   - one 2½" x 11" strip from dark brown silk for bottom binding (J)
   - one 11" x 13½" piece from cream wool for backing

3. Interface those fabrics that need a bit more body. Note: Some of the lighter weight fabrics will be more manageable if interfaced.

## CREATING THE JOURNAL AREA

1. Print words you wish to journal from a computer. Using permanent ink pen that is similar to embroidery floss, transfer lettering onto right side of fabric (F). Heat-set ink with iron. Another option would be to transfer the journaling onto fabric, using ink-jet transfer paper. Refer to **Journaling on Fabric** pages 48–49. You may simply wish to handwrite your journaling with a fabric writing pen or fabric paint.

2. Backstitch journaling with three strands of embroidery floss. Note: Embroidered journaling must be done prior to piecing the page together.

## CREATING THE LOTUS BLOSSOM BLOCK

Finished size: 4"

1. Refer to **Foundation Piecing** on pages 15–17. Using **Foundation-piecing Patterns** on page 69, trace two of **Unit 1** onto nonwoven interfacing. Trace two of **Unit 2** onto nonwoven interfacing.

2. Make Lotus Blossom from silk and satin variations. Sew pieces to the foundation in numerical order.

3. Stitch Unit 1 to Unit 2 along center for Lotus Blossom, matching teal dots. See **Assembled Section Diagram** below. Repeat for remaining pieces.

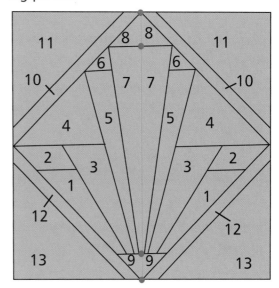

Assembled Section Diagram

## ASSEMBLING THE SCRAPBOOK PAGE

1. Sew page together in alphabetical order. See **Scrapbook Page Diagram** below. Begin by sewing assembled Lotus Blossom to left and right sides of A. Stitch D to bottom of Lotus Blossom. Pin photograph so that it overlaps and is centered on A/D. Sew E to lower edge of D, catching photo in seam line while sewing. Using decorative machine-embroidery stitch, sew other edges of photo in place. Sew F to top of Lotus Blossom.

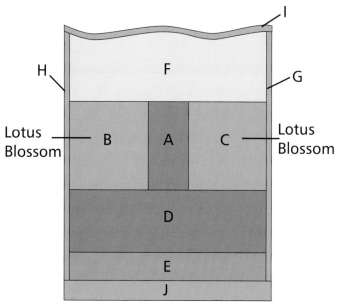

Scrapbook Page Diagram

2. Place scrapbook page on top of backing fabric, wrong sides facing. Bind side edges of page with G & H strips. Bind lower edge of page with J strip.

3. Trim upper edge of F to a curved shape. Cut three 3" lengths from ribbon. Fold in half, matching cut ends. Pin ribbon ends to top edge of F on backing near side edges and at center.

4. Bind top edge of page with I strip. Press ribbon toward binding and tack ribbon to binding.

## CREATING THE BLINZES

1. Cut two 8" squares from peach organza. See Blinzes on page 69. Follow Steps 1–4. Repeat once for two blinzes.

2. Appliqué blinzes in place.

## FINISHING THE SCRAPBOOK PAGE

1. Make two bead bangles from seed and leaf-shaped beads for center of blinzes. Refer to **Bead Dangles** on page 14.

2. Stitch bead dangles to center of blinzes.

3. Bead E section by drawing curved-stemmed shapes onto space. Sew one or two leaves to fabric at end of stem. Slip several seed beads and firepolish bead onto needle, then stitch into fabric along stem line. Backstitch through beads and slip several seed beads and a firepolish bead onto needle, stitching into fabric again along stem line. Continue in this manner to bead each stem.

4. Insert dowel or rod.

# FOLDING TECHNIQUE DIRECTIONS

## BLINZES

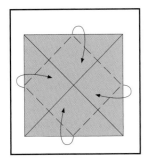 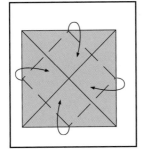 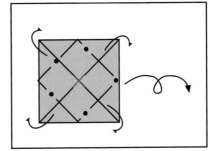 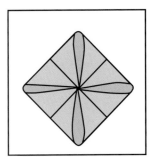

1. Press crosswise. With fabric wrong side up, fold corners to center, press at edges.

2. Repeat Step 1 at left with the new corners. Repeat this step one more time.

3. Repeat Step 1 at left with the new corners. Tack center points.

4. Turn piece over. Fold corners to center and tack at center.

## LOTUS BLOSSOM DESIGN
## FOUNDATION-PIECING PATTERNS

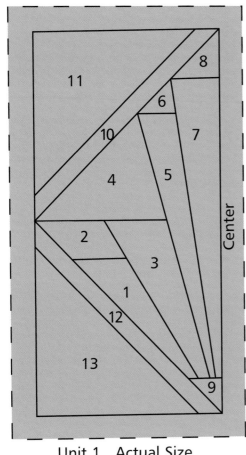 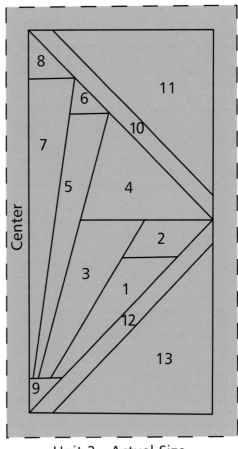

Unit 1   Actual Size          Unit 2   Actual Size

# SCALLOP DESIGN

## FABRICS:

### Brown (two variations)
- Brown linen (⅛ yd) for side bindings (H & I)
- Brown silk (⅜ yd) for backing

### Gold (three variations)
- Cream/gold striped tussah dupioni (⅛ yd) for top section (D)
- Gold cross-dyed taffeta (⅛ yd) for folded rose section (C)
- Gold velvet (⅛ yd) for top binding (J)

### Green (one variation)
- Green dupioni (⅛ yd) for side sections (E & F)

### Red (one variation)
- Dark red dupioni (scraps) for bottom binding (K)

### Silver (one variation)
- Silver silk (¼ yd) for journal section (G) and photo section (B)

### Tan (four variations)
- Four variations of tan velvet (⅛ yd) for scallop (A)

### Taupe (two variations)
- Brownish taupe organza (⅛ yd) two for diagonal folded rose
- Taupe matelassé (⅛ yd) for scallop (A)

### Terra-cotta (four variations)
- Four variations of terra-cotta silk (⅛ yd) for scallop (A)

## NOTIONS:

- **Standard Tools & Notions** on page 8
- ⅛"-wide olive green satin cord (36")
- Beading needle
- Beads:
  11/0 green seed (8)
  6mm brown pearl (6)
- Buttons:
  ½" dia. greenish gold (2)
  1" dia. greenish gold
- Canvas photo fabric (8½" x 11" sheet)
- Embroidery flosses:
  light olive
  olive
  rust
- Lightweight fusible interfacing (¼ yd)
- Nonwoven interfacing (not fusible) (¼ yd)
- Permanent ink gel pens: shades close to floss colors
- Photo
- Size 3 embroidery needle
- Wooden dowel or rod

## CREATING THE SCRAPBOOK PAGE

1. Photocopy photo onto canvas photo fabric, following manufacturer's instructions. Crop or tear photo to 2" x 4¼".

2. Cut fabrics as follows:
   - one 4¼" square from silver tussah fabric for photo center (B)
   - one 1⅞" x 8¼" strip from gold cross-dyed taffeta for diagonal folded rose section (C)
   - one 2" x 8¼" strip from cream/gold striped silk for top section (D)
   - two 1½" x 7⅜" strips from green dupioni for side sections (E & F)
   - one 5⅛" x 10¾" piece from silver silk for journal area (G)
   - two 1½" x 12½" pieces from brown linen for side bindings (H & I)
   - one 2½" x 11" strip from gold velvet for top binding (J)
   - one 2½" x 11" strip from rust dupioni for bottom binding (K)

3. Interface those fabrics that need a bit more body. Note: Some of the lighter weight fabrics will be more manageable if interfaced.

## CREATING THE JOURNAL AREA

1. Print words you wish to journal from a computer, then transfer lettering onto right side of fabric (G). Another option would be to transfer the journaling onto fabric, using inkjet transfer paper. Refer to **Journaling the Fabric** on pages 48–49. You may simply wish to handwrite your journaling with a fabric writing pen or fabric paint.

2. Backstitch journaling with three strands of embroidery floss. Note: Embroidered journaling must be done prior to piecing the page together.

## CREATING THE SCALLOP

Finished size: 4"

1. Refer to **Foundation Piecing** on pages 15–17. Using **Foundation-piecing Patterns** on page 75, trace **Unit 1** onto nonwoven interfacing. Trace **Unit 2** onto nonwoven interfacing.

2. Make Scallop from satin and velvet fabric variations. Sew pieces to foundation in numerical order.

3. Sew Unit 1 to Unit 2 along center for Scallop. See **Assembled Scallop Diagram** below.

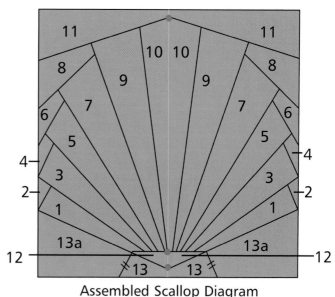

Assembled Scallop Diagram

## ASSEMBLING THE SCRAPBOOK PAGE

1. Sew page together in alphabetical order. See **Scrapbook Page Diagram** below. Begin by pinning the 2" x 4¼" cropped or torn photo to fabric B piece along upper and lower edges. Sew assembled scallop to left edge of B. Sew C to bottom edge of scallop/photo section. Sew D to top edge of scallop/photo section. Sew E and F to left and right edges of complete upper section. Sew G to bottom of upper section.

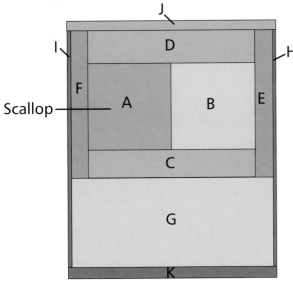

Scrapbook Page Diagram

2. Place scrapbook page on top of backing fabric, wrong sides facing. Bind side edge of page with H and I strips. Bind bottom edge of page with K strip.

3. Fold top binding (J) in half lengthwise, right sides facing. Sew short ends, turn piece right side out and press. Sew raw edge of rod-pocket binding to right side of top edge. Press seam allowance toward rod-pocket binding. Fold rod-pocket binding over to back side and onto seam. Stitch in place, leaving side edges open.

4. Insert dowel or rod.

## CREATING THE DIAGONAL FOLDED ROSE

1. Cut two 2" x 18" strips from brownish taupe silk organza fabric.

2. See **Diagonal-folded Rose** on page 74. Follow Steps 1–4 to make one rose. Repeat once for two diagonal-folded roses.

## TIP:

The Diagonal-folded Rose is most effective when worked on sheer silk fabric, lightweight silk fabric, or ribbon. An 18" length forms a 1¼"-wide rose.

## FINISHING THE SCRAPBOOK PAGE

1. Stitch folded roses in place as shown in photo on page 71.

2. Stitch one button onto each side and at center of folded rose.

3. Take a few gathering stitches at center of side edges of G. With doubled thread, slip three pearls onto beading needle, each alternated with a seed bead. Stitch group of beads around gathered edge.

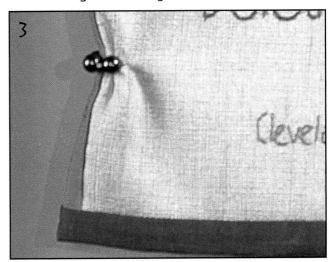

# FOLDING TECHNIQUE DIRECTIONS

## DIAGONAL-FOLDED ROSE

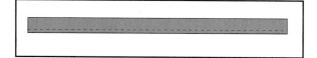

1. Fold in half lengthwise, right sides facing and using ¼" seam allowance. Press seam allowance open and turn right side out. Flatten, with seam along bottom edge.

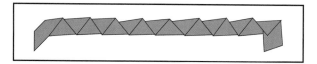

2. Press strip back and forth diagonally, forming continuous mountains, having depth of diagonal folds ½" and so that strip ends at same folded edge.

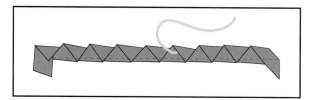

3. Sew along bottom edge as shown. Using large-eyed needle, insert a narrow cord into top of each fold, slightly gathering top edge in the process. Stitch cord at each end to secure.

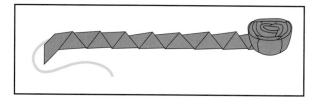

4. Roll piece along bottom edge into a rose shape. Repeat Steps 1–4 for a total of two roses.

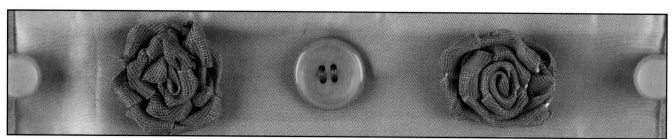

Finished Diagonal-folded Rose

# SCALLOP DESIGN FOUNDATION-PIECING PATTERNS

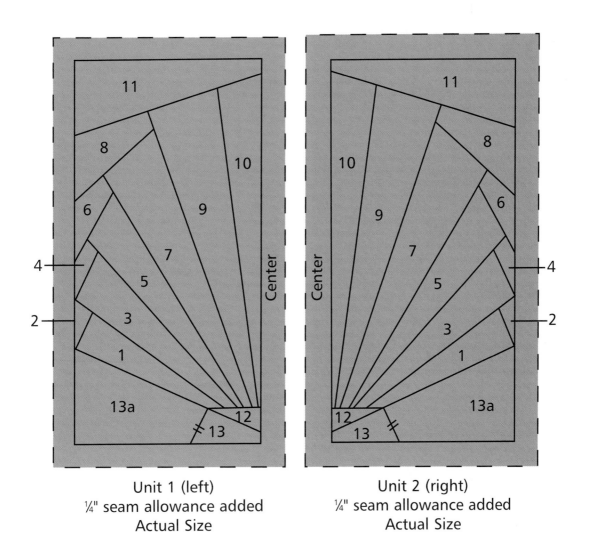

Unit 1 (left)
¼" seam allowance added
Actual Size

Unit 2 (right)
¼" seam allowance added
Actual Size

# SOLOMON'S TEMPLE DESIGN

## FABRICS:

### Brown (four variations)
- Dark brown silk (⅛ yd) for bottom section (E)
- Three variations of brown satin and velvet (⅛ yd) for Solomon's Temple (A) and Bachelor Button (D)

### Gold (one variation)
- Cream/gold striped silk (⅛ yd) for side bindings (I & J)

### Green (six variations)
- Chartreuse silk (⅛ yd) for Solomon's Temple (A)
- Green dupioni (⅛ yd) for sides (G & H) and top section (F)
- Teal washable wool (⅛ yd) for bottom binding (K)
- Three variations of green silk (⅛ yd) for Bachelor Button (D)

### Red (one variation)
- Dark red dupioni (scrap) for top binding (L)

### Tan (five variations)
- Four variations of tan satin and velvet (⅛ yd each) for Solomon's Temple (A), Bachelor Button (D)
- Tan wool (10½" x 13") for backing
- Tan velvet (⅛ yd) for bow

### Taupe (four variations)
- Brownish taupe organza (⅛ yd) for tailored bow
- Greenish taupe dupioni for photo/journal areas (B & C)
- Two variations of taupe silk (⅛ yd each) for Solomon's Temple (A)

### Terra-cotta (four variations)
- Four variations of satin and velvet (⅛ yd each) for Bachelor Button (D)

## NOTIONS:

- **Standard Notions & Tools** on page 8
- ⅜"-dia. or smaller buttons: lavender tan (4 assorted)
- 1¼" bow-shaped button
- ⅝"-wide dark red taffeta ribbon (9")
- Beading needle
- Beads: 3mm round gold (3) 6mm round green pearl 8mm round green variegated
- Canvas photo fabric (8½" x 11" sheet)
- Lightweight fusible interfacing (¼ yd)
- Nonwoven interfacing (not fusible) (¼ yd)
- Olive green embroidery floss
- Permanent ink fabric writing pen
- Photo
- Size 3 embroidery needle
- Wooden dowel or rod

## CREATING THE SCRAPBOOK PAGE

1. Photocopy photos onto canvas photo fabric, following manufacturer's instructions. Crop or tear photos so they are less than 3½" square.

2. Cut fabrics as follows:
   - two 4" squares from greenish taupe dupioni for photograph section (B) and journal section (C)

Continued on page 78.

Continued from page 76.

- one 2" x 7½" piece from dark brown silk for bottom section (E)
- one 4" x 7" piece from green dupioni for top section (F)
- two 2" x 12" strips from green dupioni fabric for side sections (G & H)
- two 1½" x 12" strips from cream/gold striped silk for side bindings (I & J)
- one 2" x 9½" strip from teal fabric for bottom binding (K)
- one 1½" x 16" strip from dark red dupioni for top binding (L)

3. Interface those fabrics that need a bit more body. Note: Some of the lighter weight fabrics will be more manageable if interfaced.

## CREATING THE JOURNAL AREA

1. Print words you wish to journal from a computer, then transfer lettering onto the right edge of B fabric piece and the left edge of C fabric piece on the right side of the fabric. Heat-set ink with an iron. Another option would be to transfer the journaling onto fabric, using ink-jet transfer paper. Refer to **Journaling on the Fabric** on pages 48–49. You may simply wish to handwrite your journaling with a fabric writing pen or fabric paint.

2. Backstitch journaling with three strands of embroidery floss. Note: Embroidered journaling must be done prior to piecing the page together.

## CREATING THE SOLOMON'S TEMPLE

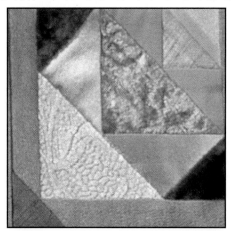

1. Refer to **Foundation Piecing** on pages 15–17. Using **Foundation-piecing Pattern** on page 81, trace **Unit 1** onto nonwoven interfacing.

2. Make Solomon's Temple from silk and velvet variations. Sew pieces to foundation in numerical order.

## CREATING THE BACHELOR BUTTON

1. Using Foundation-piecing patterns on page 81, trace **Unit 2** onto nonwoven interfacing. Trace **Unit 3** onto nonwoven interfacing.

2. Make Bachelor Button from silk and velvet variations. Sew pieces to foundation in numerical order.

3. Sew Unit 2 to Unit 3 for Bachelor Button. See **Assembled Bachelor Button** diagram below.

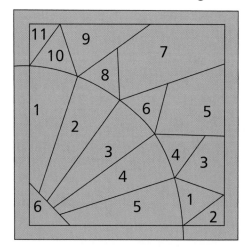

Assembled Bachelor Button Diagram

## ASSEMBLING THE SCRAPBOOK PAGE

1. Stitch page together in alphabetical order. See **Scrapbook Page Diagram** below. Begin by sewing left edge of assembled Solomon's temple (A) to right edge of B. Sew left edge of C to right edge of assembled Bachelor Button. Sew A/B to C/D, forming center section. Sew F to top of center section Sew E to bottom of center section. Sew G and H to sides of center section. Stitch photos to B and C, overlapping photo edges onto the other sections, as desired.

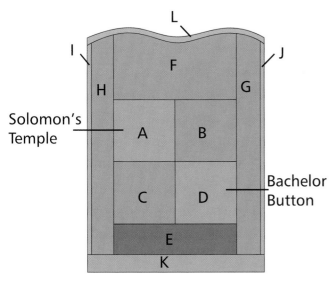

Scrapbook Page Diagram

2. Place scrapbook page on top of backing fabric, wrong sides facing. Bind side edge of page with I and J strips. Bind bottom edge of page with K strip, stitching cut edge of K to front and back of page along bottom edge. Sew side edges together.

3. Trim upper edge of F to a curved shape. Cut three 3" lengths from ribbon. Fold in half, matching cut ends. Pin ribbon ends to top edge of F on backing near side edges and at center.

4. Bind top edge of page with L strip, extending strip off page on both sides. Press ribbon toward binding and tack ribbon to binding. Tie a knot with binding where binding extends off page on both sides. Trim binding just past knot with a diagonal cut.

## CREATING THE MULTILAYER TAILORED BOW

1. Cut 4¼" x 49" strip from brownish taupe silk organza.

2. Make one bow. See **Multilayer Tailored Bow** on page 80. Follow Steps 1–4.

## FINISHING THE SCRAPBOOK PAGE

1. Appliqué multilayered tailored bow centered onto F, leaving upper bow layers untacked.

2. Use embroidery floss to pleat-gather center of bottom binding (K). Stitch a bead dangle onto center of bottom binding (K), using 8mm and 6mm beads, alternated with 3mm beads.

3. Stitch buttons onto Bachelor Button as shown in photo on page 77.

4. Stitch bow-shaped button below photo section (C).

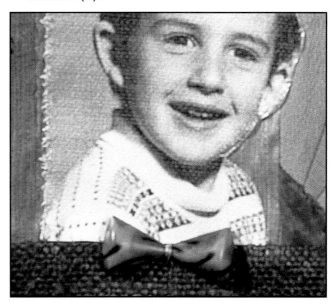

5. Insert dowel or rod.

# FOLDING TECHNIQUE DIRECTIONS

## MULTILAYERED TAILORED BOW

1. Press long edges over to fabric wrong side, forming 1¾"-wide strip of fabric.

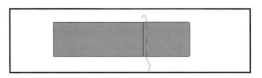

2. Cut 16" strip from brownish taupe organza. Fold strip to form bottom layer of bow, off-setting center.

3. Form two more layers to bow, having each layer ½" shorter in length than previous layer. Make one more half-layer for bow. Gather-stitch across bow center.

4. Cover center with a folded-over strip of velvet, tacking ends on bow back side.

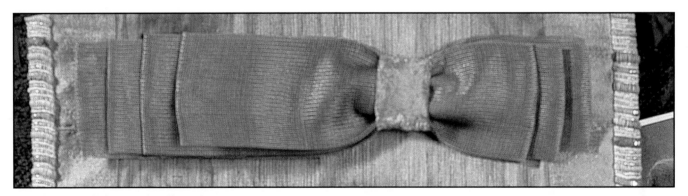

Finished Multilayered Tailored Bow

# SOLOMON'S TEMPLE DESIGN FOUNDATION-PIECING PATTERNS

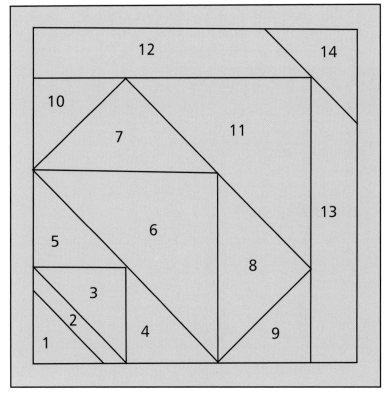

Unit 1
Actual Size

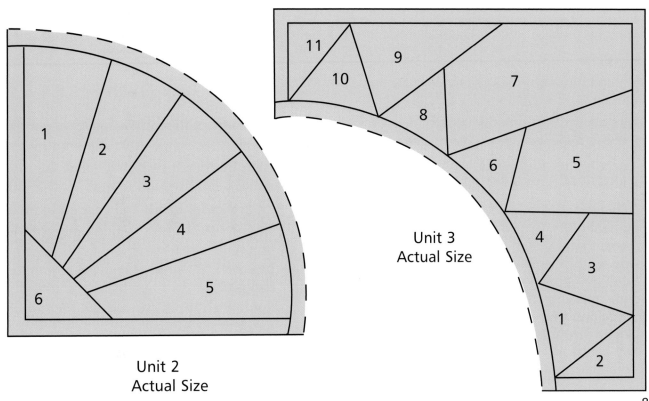

Unit 2
Actual Size

Unit 3
Actual Size

# BANDED BROKEN DISHES PILLOW

## FABRICS:

Note: All fabrics are a minimum of 42" wide.

Black Quilting Cotton (one variation)
• Black floral (⅛ yd) for A

Gold (three variations)
• Cream/gold brocade (⅛ yd) for C
• Gold patterned quilting cotton (⅛ yd) for A
• Gold plaid cotton (½ yd) for D

Olive Quilting Cotton (two variations)
• Light olive tone-on-tone (⅛ yd) for A
• Olive swirl (⅛ yd) for A

Purple (one variation)
• Grayish purple silk striped (½ yd) for E and backing

Red (one variation)
• Reddish orange (¼ yd) for B

## NOTIONS:

• **Pillow Tools & Notions** on page 9
• **Standard Tools & Notions** on page 8
• 16" pillow form
• ½" dia. buttons (3)

## DEFINING THE PROJECT

Three of the five pillows featured in this book on pages 82–103 use four individual folded elements that are then overlapped. Once overlapped, the elements are entwined. The effect of these overlapped and entwined elements is quite amazing and form the central focus point for pillows that are trained toward classic quilt blocks. A fourth pillow also employs overlapped and entwined triangles in an effective but simpler approach. The fifth pillow makes the cathedral window come alive. Cottons, silks, and brocade fabrics are combined within each depiction.

## CREATING OVERLAPPING AND ENTWINED ELEMENTS

Folding technique: Banded Edge with Points Drawn to Center

Finished size: 16" square

1. Cut one 4¼" x 12¼" piece from each of the following fabrics:
   • black floral
   • gold patterned
   • light olive
   • olive swirl

2. Cut four 5¼" x 12¼" pieces from plaid cotton.

3. Create folded center section. Sew a plaid piece to each quilting cotton piece, aligning longer edges, using ¼" seam allowance. See **Banded Edge with Points Drawn to Center** on page 87. Follow Steps 1–4. Trim assembled piece so it is square.

## CREATING THE PILLOW

Note: Enlarge pattern 200% unless otherwise indicated.

1. Using **Triangle B** pattern on page 87, cut four triangles from reddish orange brocade (B).

2. Cut fabrics for bands and backing as follows:
   • two 4" x 10¼" pieces from cream/gold brocade for bands (C)
   • two 2¾" x 17" strips from plaid cotton for bands (D)
   • two 12" x 17" pieces from grayish purple silk for band (E) and backing

3. Sew pieces in place with a **Continuous Overlap**, using the following method:

a. Using ⅜" seam allowance, sew triangles around folded center section (A). Note: The triangles are stitched with a continuous overlap and the triangle itself is larger than an edge of folded center section. Mark centers of triangles at long diagonal edges and mark centers of edges of folded center section. Match centers of diagonal edges to center-section edges with right sides facing.

b. When sewing first triangle in place, begin 1" away from upper edge. Sew seam, press toward triangle. Sew second triangle to next adjacent seam, matching centers, but this time beginning sewing where second triangle overlaps the first at outermost edge. Repeat with next adjacent side.

c. At the fourth side, lift first triangle when sewing seam so that it is not caught accidentally in seam. Replace first triangle over last and complete first seam. Trim piece to 12¼" square.

## FINISHING THE PILLOW

1. Sew bands (C) to top and bottom edges, right sides facing, using ⅜" seam allowance. Press seam allowance toward bands. Sew bands (D) to side edges, using ⅜" seam allowance. See **Pillow Front Diagram** at right. Press seam allowance toward bands.

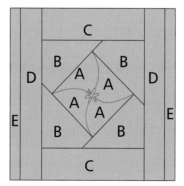

Pillow Front Diagram

2. For this pillow, the outermost side bands also fold over to become pillow backs. Press longer edges of each pillow back under 1" to wrong side. Press edges under again 1" to wrong side. Stitch-hem in place, close to inner folded edge.

3. Work buttonholes along one hemmed edge. Make buttonholes ⅛" larger than button size. Use as many buttons as desired and equally space buttonholes along hemmed edge.

4. Sew hemmed bands/backs (E) to side edges of bands (D), right sides facing, using ⅜" seam allowance. See **Pillow Front Diagram** at lower left.

5. Fold extended backs over front, right sides facing. Place the buttonholed back in place first over the front, aligning the top and bottom edges. Overlap second back over first back at hemmed edges and align top and bottom edges. Pin and sew top and bottom edges, using ½" seam allowance. Clip bulk from corners and press seam allowances open as much as possible. Turn right side out.

6. Stitch buttons in place. Slip pillow form into pillow, then button closed.

# FOLDING TECHNIQUE DIRECTIONS

## THE BASIC FOLD

 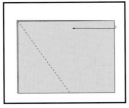 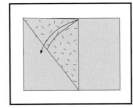 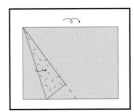

1. Fold rectangle in half lengthwise, right sides facing. With fold along top edge, stitch right edge seam with ¼" seam allowance. Clip corner, press seam allowance open. Turn right side out.

2. Place piece so that seamed edge is at left and folded edge is toward you. Fold right edge over onto left edge; press.

3. Fold left-bottom corner of the top layer up to top edge. Press and unfold.

4. Fold left-bottom corner of top layer up to creased press line; press. Turn piece over.

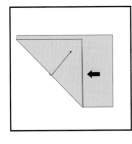 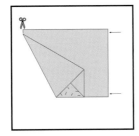 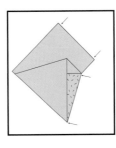 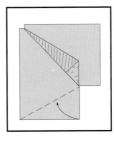 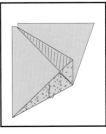

5. Folded edge continues to be placed toward you. Fold left-bottom corner up so that diagonal fold aligns with underneath layer. Fold; press.

6. Open and flatten triangle that was formed in Step 5 at left; press. Snip upper-left fold to upper point of flattened triangle.

7. Lift top layer so that the new diagonal fold aligns with the underneath layer. Fold; press.

8. Fold top layer back down and align diagonal edge with diagonal edge created in Step 7 at left; press.

9. Fold bottom-right corner diagonally up; press. With this current side of fabric up, it is the back side of the element. Repeat Steps 1–9 on this page with three contrasting fabric pieces.

# FOLDING TECHNIQUE DIRECTIONS

## THE BASIC FOLD: OVERLAPPING & ENTWINING

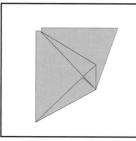

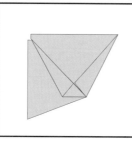

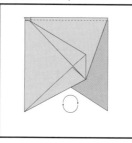

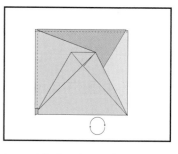

1a. With back side up, place first fabric piece so that it is positioned as shown.

1b. With back side up, place second contrasting piece in same position as in 1a, then rotate to right the next side.

2. Place upper edge of first piece over upper edge of second piece, aligning edges. Pin, then stitch along the top edges, using ⅛" seam allowance. Rotate piece to left one side.

3. With back side up, place third contrasting piece so that it is positioned same as second piece in 1b. Place upper edge of second piece over upper edge of third piece, aligning edges. Pin and stitch along top edge as with Step 2 at left. The first piece will always be on top. Rotate left.

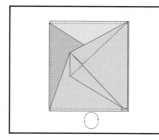

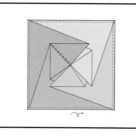

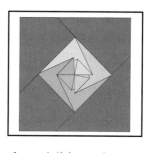

4. With back side up, place fourth contrasting piece so it is positioned as second piece in 1b above. Place upper edge of third piece over upper edge of fourth piece, aligning edges. The fourth piece will not be visible. Pin and stitch along top edge as with Step 2 above. Rotate left.

5. Entwine fourth piece with first piece so that upper edge of fourth piece is over upper edge of first piece. Pin upper edges together. Adjust, entwine and flatten center section of the four pieces. Stitch along top edge. Stitch back side center layers in place. Trim piece square. Turn piece over.

6. Invisibly tack center layers together. Stitch this piece into quilt block.

# FOLDING TECHNIQUE DIRECTIONS

## BANDED EDGE WITH POINTS DRAWN TO CENTER

 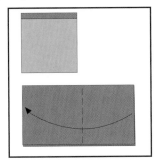 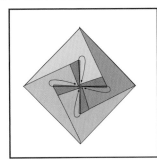 

1. Press seam allowance open. Fold fabric in half, right sides facing, having smaller piece face up. Sew right edge seam with ¼" seam allowance. Clip corner, press seam allowance open. Turn right side out.

2. Place piece with seamed edge at left and folded edge toward you. The larger piece is still facing down. See **The Basic Fold** on page 85. Follow Steps 1–8.

3. Overlap and entwine four pieces, as with **The Basic Fold, Overlapping & Entwining,** Steps 1–5 on page 86. Be certain to stitch back side centers in place to each other. Stitch front side centers in place.

4. Each element has two diagonal layers. Stitch outer folded edge of each top layer to center of square.

# BANDED BROKEN DISHES PILLOW, RUFFLED MOSAIC PILLOW, AND PLEATED PILLOW DILEMMA PATTERNS

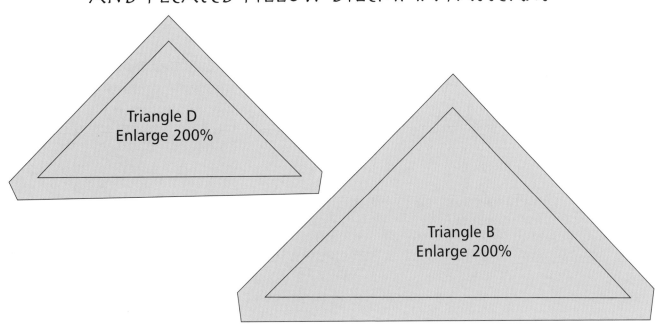

Triangle D
Enlarge 200%

Triangle B
Enlarge 200%

# RUFFLED MOSAIC PILLOW

## FABRICS:

Note: All fabrics are a minimum of 42" wide.

### Coral (one variation)
• Bright coral plaid (½ yd) for backing

### Cream (one variation)
• Cream/gold (⅛ yd) for F

### Green (five variations)
• Light olive green tone-on-tone quilting cotton (½ yd) for A and C
• Light olive green dupioni (¼ yd) for E
• Olive green floral quilting cotton (¼ yd) for A
• Olive green stripe quilting cotton (¼ yd) for A
• Olive green swirl quilting cotton (¼ yd) for A

### Red (one variation)
• Reddish orange (¼ yd) for B and D

## NOTIONS:
• **Pillow Tools & Notions** on page 9
• **Standard Tools & Notions** on page 8
• 18" pillow form
• Cover buttons:
  ½" dia.
  1⅛" dia. (2)
• Lightweight fusible interfacing (¼ yd)

## CREATING THE SLIGHTLY RUFFLED EFFECT

Folding techniques: Overlapping & Entwined
Elements: Sightly Ruffled Effect

1. Cut four 6¾" x 9¼" pieces from each of the following fabrics:
   • light olive green tone-on-tone
   • olive green floral
   • olive green stripe
   • olive green swirl

2. Create four folded sections, using one fabric for each section. See **Overlapping & Entwined Elements: Slightly Ruffled Effect** on page 91. Follow Steps 1–3. Trim (assembled piece so it is square.

## CREATING THE PATCHWORK DESIGN

Note: Enlarge pattern 200% unless otherwise indicated.

1. Using **Triangle B** pattern on page 87, cut four triangles from reddish orange brocade fabric (B).

2. Using **Triangle D** pattern on page 87, cut two triangles from reddish orange brocade fabric (D).

3. Cut fabric pieces for bands and backing as follows:
   - one 9" square from light olive green tone-on-tone for dimensional square appliqué (C over center E)
   - three 4½" squares from dupioni for side squares (E)
   - two 3⅝" x 18" pieces from cream/gold brocade for bands (F)
   - one 12½" x 18" piece and one 10½" x 18" piece from plaid for pillow back

4. Fuse interfacing to wrong side of three 4½" squares (E).

5. See **Pillow Front Diagram** below. Working first diagonal row, sew one E square to one A square. Sew one Triangle D to other side of A. For second row, sew one A square to one E square. Sew A to other side of E. For third row, sew Triangle D to A square. Sew E square to other side of A. Sew three rows together to form pillow center. Sew Triangle Bs to outer corners. When working with heavy brocade fabrics, use ⅜" seam allowance against a smaller ¼" seam allowance for cottons. Press seam allowances toward least bulky direction.

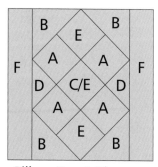

Pillow Front Diagram

## CREATING THE DIMENSIONAL SQUARE APPLIQUÉ

Folding technique: Dimension Square Appliqué

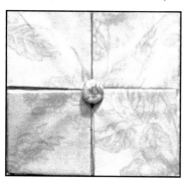

1. See **Dimensional Square Appliqué** on page 92. Fold light olive green square (C), following Steps 1–8.

2. Appliqué square in place over center of patchwork (E).

3. Using ⅜" seam allowance, sew one band (F) each to side edges. Press seam allowance toward bands.

## FINISHING THE PILLOW

1. Press longer edges of each pillow back under 1" to wrong side. Press edges under again 1" to wrong side. Stitch-hem in place close to inner folded edge.

2. Work buttonholes along one hemmed edge. Make buttonholes ⅛" larger than button size. Use as many buttons as desired and equally space buttonholes along hemmed edge.

3. Place backs over front, right sides facing. Place buttonholed back down in place first over front, aligning outer edges. Overlap second back over first back at hemmed edges and align outer edges with front. Using ½" seam allowance, sew around four sides. Clip bulk from corners and press seam allowances open as much as possible. Turn right side out.

4. Cover ½" button with cream/gold brocade. Cover 1⅛" buttons with reddish orange brocade. Refer to manufacturer's directions for covering buttons with fabric.

5. Stitch ½" button to center of dimensional square appliqué.

6. Stitch 1⅛" buttons in place within middle of hemmed edge of back without buttonholes.

7. Slip pillow form into pillow. Button closed.

# FOLDING TECHNIQUE DIRECTIONS

## OVERLAPPING & ENTWINED ELEMENTS: SLIGHTLY RUFFLED EFFECT

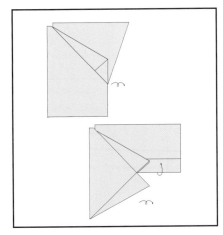

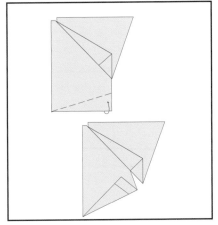

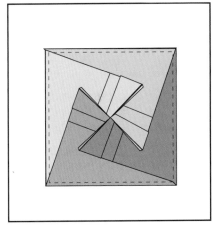

1. Refer to **The Basic Fold** on page 85. Follow Steps 1–8, then, turn element over to other side, keeping all folds in place and positioning piece as shown. Lift middle triangle layer and fold straight edge at right side up about one-fourth of whole space. Press fold very crisply, causing middle triangle layer to stand upright. Gently fold standing-up triangle flat, but do not press.

2. Turn piece over again to other side and position as shown. Fold corner indicated diagonally, tapering fold to nothing at bottom-left corner. Press well, being careful to not flatten middle triangle on other side. Repeat with three remaining pieces.

3. Overlap and entwine four pieces. Refer to **The Basic Fold, Overlapping & Entwining** on page 86. Follow Steps 1–5, making certain to stitch back side centers in place. Stitch entwined center together.

# FOLDING TECHNIQUE DIRECTIONS

## DIMENSIONAL SQUARE APPLIQUÉ

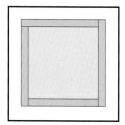 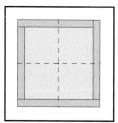 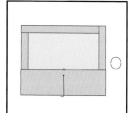 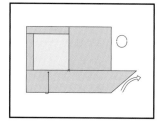

1. With wrong side up, press all edges under ½" to the wrong side.

2. Fold and press crosswise centers, wrong side up. Mark the center.

3. Press side facing inward to center fold and tack center of side to center of square. Rotate counterclockwise (up).

4. Press rotated side (side facing inward) to center fold and tack center as in Step 3 at left. Pull out excess fabric between two sides toward right. Rotate counterclockwise.

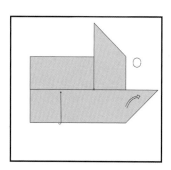 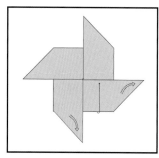 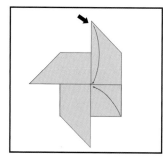 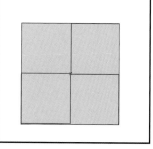

5. Repeat Step 4 above. Rotate counterclockwise.

6. Repeat Step 4 above. Pull out right excess fabric to right side. Pull out left excess fabric downward, forming a pinwheel shape.

7. Lift bottom-right triangle and flatten so that the tip is at square the center. Press.

8. Repeat with remaining three sides. Be certain to hide excess fabric that may expose itself at each tip. Tack tips to center. Appliqué piece in place.

# NORTHEAST RIDDLE PILLOW

# NORTHEAST RIDDLE PILLOW

## FABRICS:

Note: All fabrics are a minimum of 36" wide.

Cream (one variation)
• Cream/gold brocade (⅜ yd) for A

Orange (two variations)
• Orange silk brocade (⅜ yd) for A
• Reddish orange brocade (⅜ yd) for A

Purple (two variations)
• Grayish purple silk striped (⅜ yd) for A
• Purple/magenta silk brocade (¼ yd) for B

## NOTIONS:

• **Pillow Tools & Notions** on page 9
• **Standard Tools & Notions** on page 8
• Polyester stuffing (12 oz.)

### CREATING THE ELONGATED POINTS

Folding techniques: Overlapping & Entwined Elements with Elongated Points

1. Cut one 12" x 16" piece from each of the following fabrics:
   • cream/gold brocade
   • grayish purple silk striped
   • orange silk brocade
   • reddish orange brocade

2. Refer to **The Basic Fold** on page 85. Follow Steps 1–6. See **Overlapping & Entwined Elements with Elongated Points** on page 95. Follow Steps 1–5. Trim assembled piece so it is square (A). Note: These fabrics are bulky when being worked.

### ASSEMBLING THE PILLOW

1. Cut fabric pieces for bands and backing as follows:
   • four 2½" x 9½" strips from purple/magenta brocade for bands (B)
   • two 6" x 11" pieces from cream/gold brocade for backing

2. Sew pieces in place with a continuous overlap. Refer to **Continuous Overlap** on pages 82–83. Using ½" seam allowances, sew one band (B) to each edge of assembled center (A). Press seam allowances toward bands. See **Pillow Front Diagram** below.

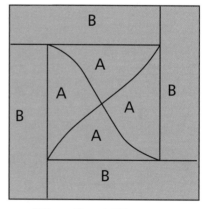

Pillow Front Diagram

## FINISHING THE PILLOW

1. Using ½" seam allowance, sew backs together along one long edge, leaving a 4" opening at center of seam. Press seam allowance open.

2. Using ½" seam allowance, pin and sew front to back. Clip bulk from corners and press seam allowances open as much as possible. Turn right side out.

3. Hand-stuff pillow with polyester stuffing through back seam opening. Slip-stitch opening closed.

# FOLDING TECHNIQUE DIRECTIONS

## OVERLAPPING & ENTWINED ELEMENTS WITH ELONGATED POINTS

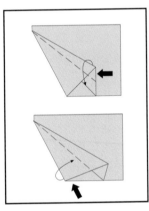 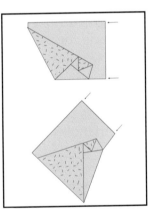 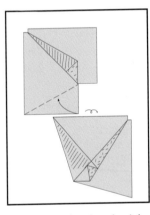 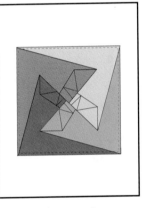

1. Open "kite" shape and fold top half of "kite" downward, aligning upper crease with center line. Press.

2. Reposition lower crease line of "kite" while accordion-pleating excess fabric on top of fold from Step 1 at left. Press. See **The Basic Fold** on page 85. Follow Steps 7–9.

3. From the back side, the element is identical to that from Step 9 of **The Basic Fold**. From the front side, the accordion-pleated space is visible. Repeat with remaining fabric pieces.

4. Overlap and entwine four pieces. Refer to **The Basic Fold, Overlapping & Entwining** on page 86. Follow Steps 1–5, making certain to sew back-side centers in place. Tack entwined center together.

# PLEATED PILLOW DILEMMA

## FABRICS:

Note: All fabrics are a minimum of 36" wide.

Orange (two variations)
• Orange silk brocade (⅛ yd) for C
• Reddish orange brocade (⅓ yd) for D

Purple (two variations)
• Grayish purple silk striped (¼ yd) for A
• Purple/magenta silk brocade (¼ yd) for B

## NOTIONS:

• **Pillow Tools & Notions** on page 9
• **Standard Tools & Notions** on page 8
• 1⅛" dia. cover button
• Polyester stuffing (24 oz.)

## CREATING THE ACCORDION PLEATED TRIANGLES

Folding technique: Overlapped & Entwined Triangles with Accordion Pleats

1. Cut four 6" squares from grayish purple silk. See **Overlapped & Entwined Triangles: The Basic Technique** on page 86. Follow Steps 1–5.

2. Accordion-pleat triangles. See **Overlapped & Entwined Triangles: Accordion Pleated** on page 98. Follow Steps 1–3. Trim assembled piece (A) so it is square.

## ASSEMBLING THE PILLOW

Note: Enlarge pattern 200% unless otherwise indicated.

1. Using **Triangle B** pattern on page 87, cut four triangles (B) from purple/magenta brocade.

2. Cut fabrics for bands and backing as follows:
   • four 1¼" x 7" strips from orange silk brocade for bands (C)
   • four 3" x 15" strips from reddish orange brocade for bands (D)
   • two 8" x 15" pieces from reddish orange brocade for backing

3. Refer to **Continuous Overlap** on pages 82–83. Using ¼" seam allowances, sew one band (C) to each edge of assembled center (A). Press seam allowances toward bands. Sew triangles (B) to outer corners in the same manner. Press seam allowances toward triangles. See **Pillow Front Diagram** below.

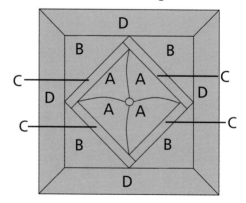

Pillow Front Diagram

4. Sew one band (D) to each outer edge, mitering bands at corners.

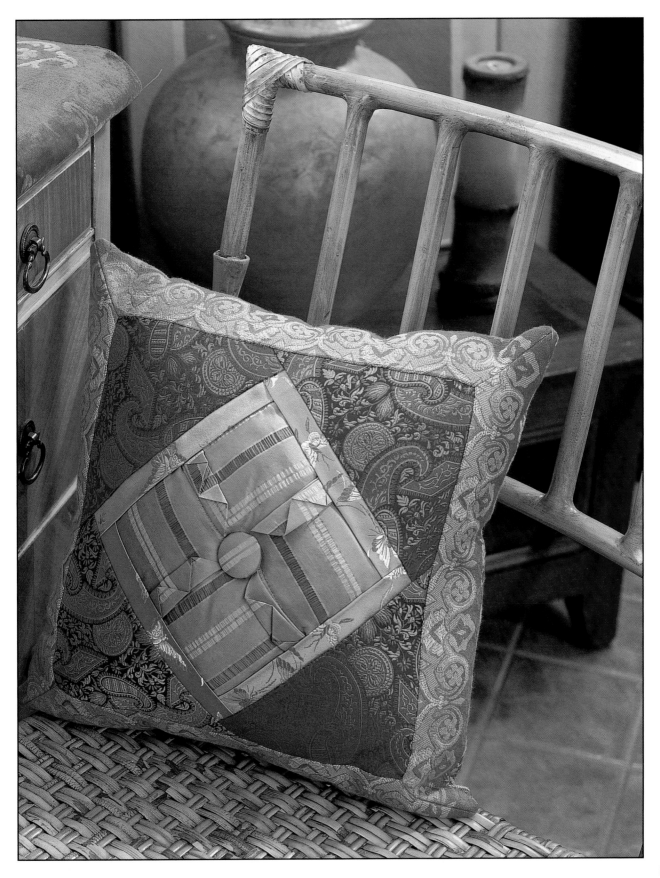

## FINISHING THE PILLOW

1. Using ½" seam allowance, sew backs together along one long edge, leaving 4" opening at center of seam. Press seam allowance open.

2. Using ½" seam allowance, pin and sew front to back. Clip bulk from corners and press seam allowances open as much as possible. Turn right side out.

3. Hand-stuff pillow with polyester stuffing through back seam opening. Slip-stitch opening closed.

4. Cover button with grayish purple silk. Refer to manufacturer's directions for covering buttons with fabric.

5. Stitch button to center of pillow.

# FOLDING TECHNIQUE DIRECTIONS

## OVERLAPPED & ENTWINED TRIANGLES: ACCORDION PLEATED

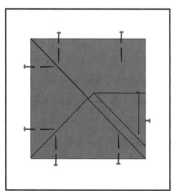
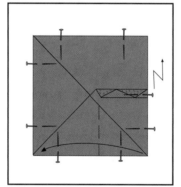
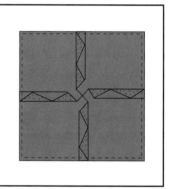

1. Find center of one side. Fold upper half of triangle over on itself ¼" above halfway mark. Press.

2. Accordion-pleat remainder of pressed-over triangle portion with ½"-deep pleats. Pin to hold.

3. Pleat remaining three sides in the same manner as Step 2 at left. Sew around four sides to hold pleats and overlaps in place.

# FOLDING TECHNIQUE DIRECTIONS

## OVERLAPPED & ENTWINED TRIANGLES: THE BASIC TECHNIQUE

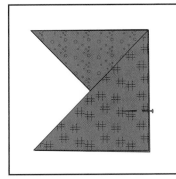

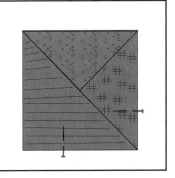

1. Press four squares diagonally in half, forming triangles.

2. Place first triangle on work surface. Place second triangle over first with folded edges toward center. Pin to hold.

3. Place third triangle over second triangle. Pin to hold.

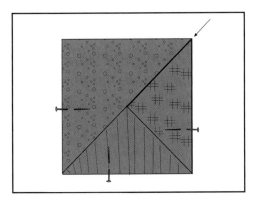

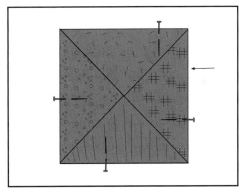

4. Place fourth triangle over third as before. Pin to hold.

5. Lift right or upper half of fourth triangle, then slip that half underneath visible half of first triangle. Pin to hold. Note: This is the completed basic shape for **Overlapped & Entwined Triangles**. Sew triangles together at center from back side.

# CATHEDRAL WINDOW PILLOW

## FABRICS:

Note: All fabrics are a minimum of 36" wide.

### Coral Quilting Cotton (one variation)
• Coral patterned (¼ yd) for Cathedral Windows

### Cream (one variation)
• Bark cloth (¼ yd) for pillow Front and Back

### Gold Quilting Cotton (two variations)
• Two variations of gold patterned (¼ yd each) for Cathedral Windows

### Orange (one variation)
• Orange silk brocade (¼ yd) for squares

### Purple (two variations)
• Grayish purple silk striped (⅛ yd) for triangles
• Purple/magenta silk brocade (¼ yd) for squares

### Rust Quilting Cotton (one variation)
• Rust patterned (¼ yd) for Cathedral Windows

## NOTIONS:
• **Pillow Tools & Notions** on page 9
• **Standard Tools & Notions** on page 8
• 1⅛" dia. button cover (2)
• 14" sq. pillow form
• Lightweight fusible interfacing (½ yd)

## CREATING THE CATHEDRAL WINDOW
Folding technique: Cathedral Window

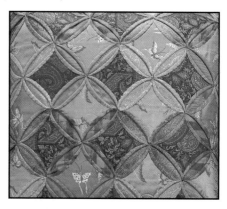

1. Cut four 8" squares each from the following fabrics for a total of 16 squares:
   • coral patterned
   • gold patterned variations
   • rust patterned

2. See **Cathedral Window** on page 103. Follow Steps 1–4 to create four 4-patch units.

3. Sew four 4-patch units together into one large square to make pillow top.

4. Cut twelve 2¼" squares each from orange and purple/magenta brocades.

5. Cut sixteen triangles from grayish purple silk, half the size of the 2¼" squares.

6. Continue, following Steps 5–6 on page 103, working orange and purple/magenta brocade squares in horizontal rows, with triangles at the outer edges.

## ASSEMBLING THE PILLOW

1. Cut fabric pieces for front and backing as follows:
   - one 15" square from bark cloth for pillow front
   - two 10" x 15" pieces from bark cloth for backing

2. Sew outer edges of Cathedral Window pillow top to bark cloth pillow front.

## FINISHING THE PILLOW

Finished size 14"

1. Press longer edges of each pillow back under 1" to wrong side. Press edges over again 1" to wrong side. Stitch-hem in place close to inner folded edge.

2. Work buttonholes along one hemmed edge. Make buttonholes ⅛" larger than button size. Equally space buttonholes along hemmed edge.

3. Place backs over front, right sides facing. Place buttonholed back in place over front, aligning outer edges. Overlap second back over first back at hemmed edges and align outer edges with front.

4. Using ½" seam allowance, sew around four sides. Clip bulk from corners and press seam allowances open as much as possible. Turn right side out.

5. Cover buttons with purple/magenta silk brocade. Refer to manufacturer's directions for covering buttons with fabric.

6. Stitch buttons in place within middle of hemmed edge of back without buttonholes.

7. Slip pillow form into pillow. Button closed.

TIP:

Square size determination for cathedral window will be 1" less in overall size, divided by two. For example, a 9" square would be 4" when finished.

9" = cut size
9" − 1" = 8"
8" ÷ 2 = 4"

4" = finished square size

# FOLDING TECHNIQUE DIRECTIONS

## CATHEDRAL WINDOW

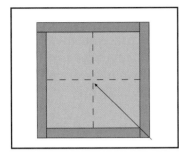

1. With wrong side up, press all edges under ½" to wrong side. Crease square cross-wise to find center.

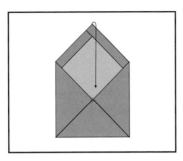

2. Fold all four corners of square to center. Tack at center. Press. When pressing, begin at the outer corners. Note: This will be helpful in creating a perfect square.

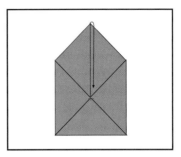

3. Fold and press four corners of new square to center. Tack corners at center together. Repeat 15 more times with the other squares for the pillow top.

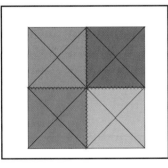

4. Machine-zigzag or ladder-stitch squares together, with matching thread. Use a different fabric for each square in the 4-patch.

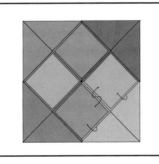

5. Place or fuse a square of contrasting fabric diagonally over seam of two squares. Repeat with each set of squares, creating horizontal pattern with contrasting fabric. The size of placed square should be a scant ⅛" smaller all around than its space.

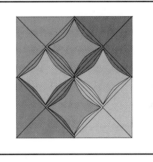

6. Fold edges of original squares over raw edges of fused squares. Invisibly stitch or machine-sew folded-over edges in place. Fuse triangles in place at outer edges. Fold edges of the original squares over raw edges of fused triangles in the same manner.

# ELEPHANT TOTE

## FABRICS:

Note: All fabrics are a minimum of 36" wide.

### Blue (four variations)
- Blue/cream striped (8" sq.) for Elephant body
- Blue/white cotton striped (¼ yd) for one Elephant body, two trunks, and lining (A)
- Blue/white plaid (8" sq.) for Elephant body
- Navy washable wool (⅛ yd) for upper Front and Back (D)

### Brown (two variations)
- Dark brown silk (⅛ yd) for lower front and back

### Green (three variations)
- Drab olive green heavy linen (¼ yd) for tote Front and Back (A)
- Green striped 2¾" x 4½" for Elephant trunk
- Teal washable wool (⅛ yd) for handles (B)

## NOTIONS:

- **Standard Tools & Notions** on page 8
- Beads:
  4mm plum round (3)
  18mm aqua oval ceramic beads (3)
- Brown embroidery floss
- Matching threads
- Polyester stuffing (handful)
- White pipe cleaner

## DEFINING THE PROJECT

The totes on pages 104–125 are a whimsical way in which to showcase your folding techniques in creating your favorites from the animal kingdom. They will surely inspire your quilting projects, whatever they may be.

## PREPARING THE PIECES

Note: Enlarge all patterns 200% unless otherwise indicated.

1. Using **Elephant Tote** pattern on page 109, cut one piece from the following fabrics, along designated line:
   - navy wool for upper Front and Back (D)
   - olive green linen for Front and Back (A)
   - two blue/white striped for Front and Back lining pieces (A)
   - two dark brown silk for lower Front and Back (C)

2. Using **Tote Bottom** pattern on page 109, cut one piece from the following fabrics:
   - blue/white striped for bottom lining piece
   - dark brown silk for bottom piece

3. Cut fabrics for tote as follows:
   - two 1½" x 11" strips from teal wool for bead strip (B)
   - two 1" x 16" strips from teal wool for handles

4. Using water-soluble fabric marker, transfer handle placement, bead placement, strip placement, and dot marks from pattern onto olive green Front and Back fabric pieces.

## ASSEMBLING THE TOTE

1. Using olive green Front and Back pieces as foundations, sew 1½" teal strip (B) to Front and Back where indicated on pattern, taking

½" seam allowance along upper line with teal strip. Press strip toward lower edge of Front and Back.

2. Sew brown pieces (C) to Front and Back in the same manner as Step 1 on page 104, catching lower edge of teal strip in with brown piece seam, using ½" seam allowance. Press strip toward lower edge of Front and Back. Align edges of brown piece to lower portion of Front and Back shape.

3. Sew navy pieces to top edge of Front and Back, using ½" seam allowance. Press seam allowance open. Sew lining Front and Back pieces to remaining long edge of navy pieces, using ½" seam allowance. Press seam allowance open.

4. Sew tote side/lining side seams, matching all striped intersections, using ½" seam allowance. Press seam allowances open.

5. Fold lining to purse inside by folding navy piece where designated on the pattern (the widest part of the tote). Topstitch around upper edge of tote ¼" from folded edge. Align outer and lining tote bottom edges. Pin edges together.

6. Layer outer and lining Bottom pieces, wrong sides facing. Pin and sew Bottoms to tote lower edge, with outer fabric right sides facing, matching dots, using ½" seam allowance. Sew again ⅛" inward from first stitched row. Trim seam allowance just past stitching and machine-overcast. Press.

## MAKING THE HANDLE

1. Fold one handle piece in half, aligning long edges. Beginning and ending 1" from ends, sew long edges together ⅛" in from cut edges. Repeat with other handle piece. Trim unstitched ends into a circular shape.

2. Using six strands of embroidery floss, whip-stitch handle ends in place on upper edge of tote where indicated on pattern.

## MAKING THE ELEPHANTS

1. Cut 8" square from fabric for elephant body. Cut 2¾" x 4½" rectangle from striped fabric for elephant trunk. See **Elephant** on pages 107–108. Follow Steps 1–12. Make three folded elephants, varying blue/white fabrics so that each elephant is different. Note: One elephant has a green striped trunk.

2. Stitch one bead to each elephant face for eye.

3. Stitch elephants to tote upper edge. Note: The elephants are facing left.

4. Stitch ceramic beads to tote front where indicated on pattern.

# FOLDING TECHNIQUE DIRECTIONS

## ELEPHANT

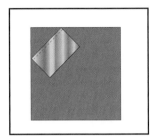

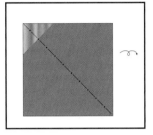

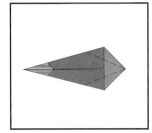

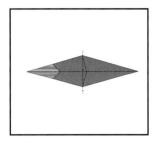

1. Mark 2½" inward from one corner on both sides, draw a line connecting marks. Position long edge of striped piece on mark and sew, using ¼" seam allowance. Press striped piece over onto corner.

2. Trim striped piece flush with corner, then trim excess fabric from 8" square at corner (underneath striped piece). Press seam allowance open.

3. Place pieced edge at left side and position square diagonally on ironing board. Press square diagonally in half to mark center, open out. Press lower-left and upper-left edges to center mark.

4. Press lower-right and upper-right edges to the center mark.

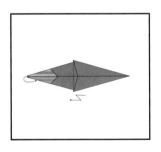

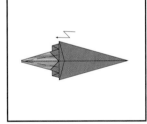

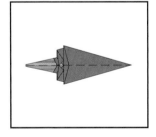

5. Turn piece over and press in half, then unfold and refold so as to form a stair-step fold. Fold left tip over about ¼" and adhere fold in place.

6. Form another stair-step fold from left side of shape.

7. Fold lower-left and upper-left edges of left tip over to center and flatten.

8. Fold piece in half, horizontally. Whip-stitch left tip together along lower edges, then insert a 1⅞" length of pipe cleaner into tip, forming bendable trunk.

Continued on page 108.

Continued from page 107.

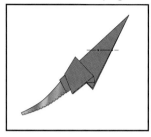 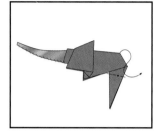  

9. Lift bottommost tips and reposition folds, forming the head and the ears.

10. Make an inside reverse fold with right tip.

11. Make another inside reverse fold with right tip in opposite direction. Coat the raw right-edge tip with a bit of fray preventative.

12. Tuck top, pointed part of head inward, tack in place. Stitch open layers closed. Stuff elephant before finishing. Tack tail to back end of elephant, then gather-stitch around tail. Lift and reposition ear fold, forming a flap. Tack ear fold in place.

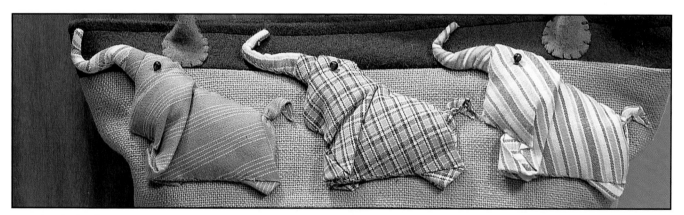

Finished Elephants

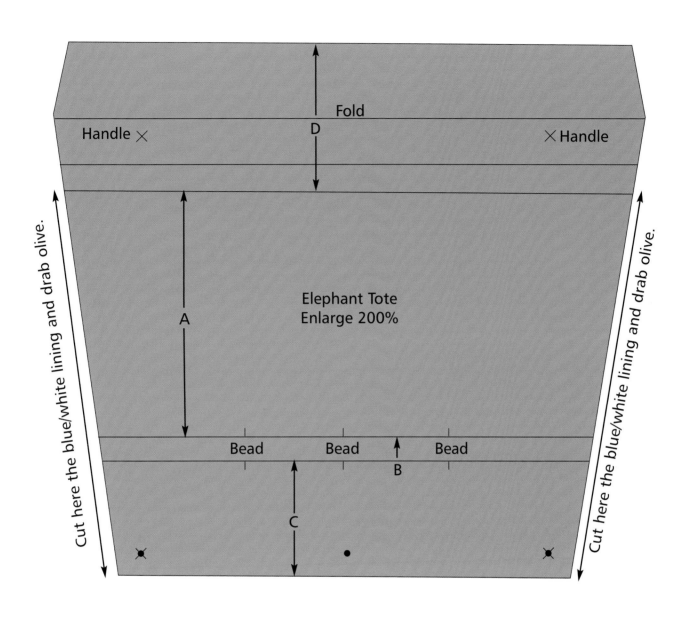

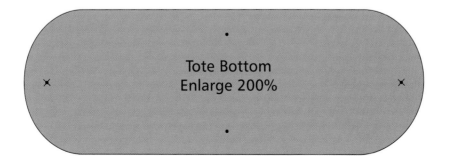

# LITTLE PIGGY TOTE

## FABRICS:

Note: All fabrics are a minimum of 36" wide.

Pink (five variations)
- Pink/brown large-sized plaid (¼ yd) for body (D)
- Pink/brown small-sized plaid (¼ yd) for snout, tail, and Flap/Pocket (C & E)
- Pink on brown striped (⅛ yd) for Legs (A)
- Pink on cream print (⅛ yd) for Toes (B) and handle
- Pink wool felt (1" scrap) for eye

## NOTIONS:

- **Standard Tools & Notions** on page 8
- ½" dia. decorative pearl snap
- Brown embroidery floss
- Lightweight fusible interfacing (½ yd)
- Matching threads
- Polyester stuffing (handful)
- Small bead

## PREPARING THE PIECES

Note: Enlarge patterns 200% unless otherwise indicated.

1. Cut fabrics as follows:
   - one 8" x 16" piece from large-sized plaid for body (D)
   - two 4¼" x 8" pieces from small-sized plaid for face and tail (C)
   - one 1¼" x 44" strip from print fabric for handle

2. Using **Flap/Pocket** pattern on page 115, cut two Flap/Pocket pieces from small-sized plaid (E).

3. Using **Leg** pattern on page 115, cut four legs from striped fabric (A),

4. Using **Toe** pattern on page 115, cut four toes from print fabric (B).

5. Fuse interfacing onto back side of body (D). Fuse interfacing onto back side of one Flap/ Pocket (E).

## CREATING THE PIGGY

1. Sew each B to each A along diagonal edges, right sides facing, using ¼" seam allowance. Press seam allowances open. Sew one C between to assembled A/B's. Press seam allowances open. Sew D to one side of each assembled A/B/C. Press seam allowances open. See **Pig Patchwork Diagram** below.

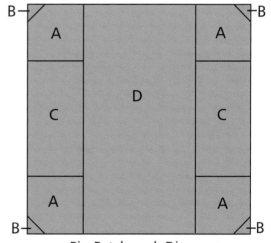

Pig Patchwork Diagram

2. Press all outer edges under ½" to wrong side.

3. See **Piggy** on page 113. Follow Steps 1–5.

4. Make Flap/Pocket. Pin and sew two Flap/Pocket pieces together, right sides facing, using ¼" seam allowance, leaving opening along lower edge where indicated on pattern. Trim bulk from corners and edge-press seam allowances open. Turn right side out. Press flat.

5. Open out piece, as shown in the **Pocket Diagram** below.

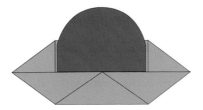

Pocket Diagram

6. Fold upper layer of large triangles over to reveal center space on one-half of opened-out piece. Position Flap/Pocket so that it is centered in the space between side triangles, having Flap/Pocket straight edge approximately ⅛" upward from center line. Sew Flap/Pocket in place along side and lower edges through two layers of center space. Refold piece so that it looks like Step 5 on page 113.

7. Proceed with **Piggy**, Steps 6–11 on pages 113–114.

8. Fold flap over top edge of piggy and onto piggy front. Press in place. Mark Flap and piggy front for snap placement. Attach snap to right side of Flap and front, following manufacturer's instructions.

## MAKING THE HANDLE

1. Press long edges of handle strip over ¼" to wrong side, then press piece in half again lengthwise.

2. Topstitch along both long edges. Tie a knot at each handle end, then stitch knot to inside sides of piggy's open space.

## FINISHING THE TOTE

1. Cut small oval as desired from felt. Whipstitch onto face.

2. Stitch bead onto oval for eye.

# FOLDING TECHNIQUE DIRECTIONS

## PIGGY

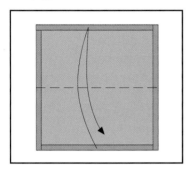

1. Press edges of fabric under ½".

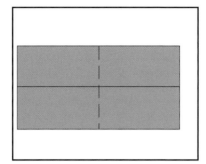

2. Press piece in half, unfold. Press upper and lower edges to center.

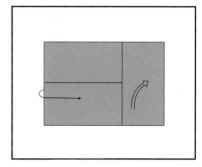

3. Press side edges to center.

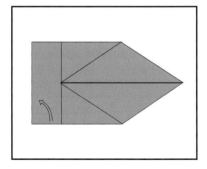

4. At center, pull upper layer out. Flatten, forming a diamond shape. Repeat with other side.

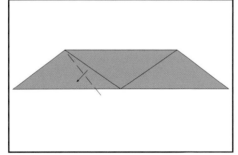

5. Press piece in half, having wider edge positioned at bottom. Sew tote Pocket/Flap in place. Refer to **Creating the Piggy** on page 112. Follow Steps 4–7 for placement.

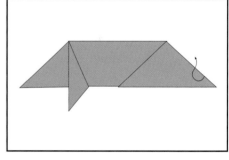

6. Working with left side, press right edge of triangular layer over. Turn over and repeat with opposite side. Turn piece over to original positioning.

Continued on page 114.

Continued from page 113.

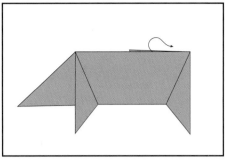

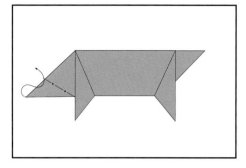

7. Push right edge of right triangles inward as with an inside reverse fold. Align inside edges of inward fold with top edges. Press, forming back legs.

8. Pull inward triangle outward in another reverse fold to form tail. Press.

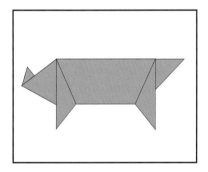

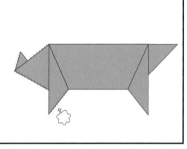

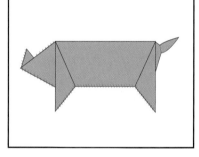

9. Make an inside reverse fold with left side tip to form snout.

10. Finish head, snout, front legs. Fill face area with a small amount of stuffing. Whipstitch upper and lower edges of face closed, along with front edge of snout. Fold front legs back and machine-sew along inner leg fold. Fill outermost layer of leg with a small amount of stuffing. Tuck tip of front leg under, then whipstitch foot area closed. Repeat for outermost front leg on opposite side, but do not stuff this leg.

11. Finish body, back legs and tail. Whipstitch lower edge of body layers together. Tack leg fold in place. This is invisibly stitched through all layers in order to create a closed space for inside of tote. Stuff outermost layer leg and finish both legs as in Step 10 at left. Gather-stitch tail, then stitch it to top-right corner. Stitch innermost layers invisibly to tote front.

# LITTLE PIGGY TOTE PATTERNS

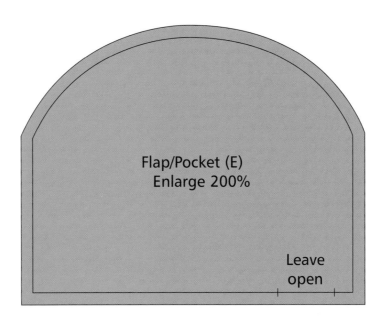

Flap/Pocket (E)
Enlarge 200%

Leave
open

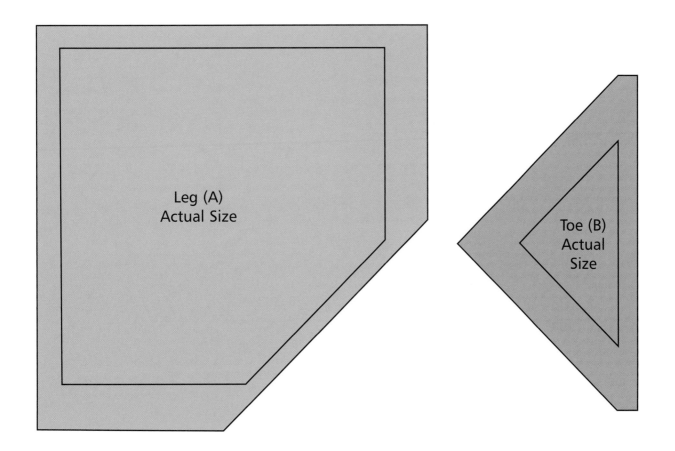

Leg (A)
Actual Size

Toe (B)
Actual
Size

# PENGUIN TOTE

## FABRICS:

Note: All fabrics are a minimum of 36" wide.

Black (one variation)
• Black plaid cotton (7½" x 8") for penguin

Blue (three variations)
• Baby blue washable wool or felt (3" x 17½") for striped body
• Light blue dot cotton (7" x 7½") for penguin lining
• Periwinkle blue wool felt (seven 1½" sq.)

Cream (two variations)
• Cream washable wool or felt (3" x 17½") for striped body
• Cream short-haired faux fur (¼ yd) for bottom binding and top band

Green (three variations)
• Light green flannel (⅜ yd) for lining
• Olive green washable wool or felt (3" x 17½") for striped body
• Teal green washable wool (3" x 17½" and ¼ yd) for base

Red (one variation)
• Brick red washable wool or felt (3" x 17½") for striped body

## NOTIONS:

• **Standard Tools & Notions** on page 8
• 5⁄16" sq. studs (7)
• 3⁄16" dia. round studs (21)
• ⅛"-wide blue satin cord (60")
• 5½" dia. circle of heavy cardboard
• 4mm plum round bead
• Matching threads
• Polyester stuffing (handful)
• Silver grommets (10)

## PREPARING THE PIECES

1. Cut 6"-diameter circle for base from each of the following fabrics:
   • light green flannel
   • teal wool fabric

2. Cut one 11" x 17½" piece from light green flannel for lining.

3. Cut one 1¼" x 17½" strip and one 4" x 17½" piece from cream short-haired faux fur.

## MAKING THE TOTE

1. To form striped body of tote, seam five 3" x 17½" strips together, using ½" seam allowance. Press seam allowances open. See photo on opposite page for color placement.

2. Position periwinkle blue squares haphazardly, but somewhat evenly spaced, along top strip. Sew squares in place crosswise. Attach one square stud in center of each small square.

3. Using disappearing-ink fabric marker, draw dashed line in the form of a simple wave pattern along the lower three strips, then attach studs in place along wave, spacing them 1" apart.

4. Fold striped tote body piece in half, right sides facing, aligning and matching striped seam lines. Sew edges, using ½" seam allowance. Press seam allowance open. Turn piece right side out.

5. Fold lining piece in half, right sides facing, aligning short edges. Sew edges, using ½" seam allowance. Press seam allowance open. Do not turn right side out.

Continued on page 118.

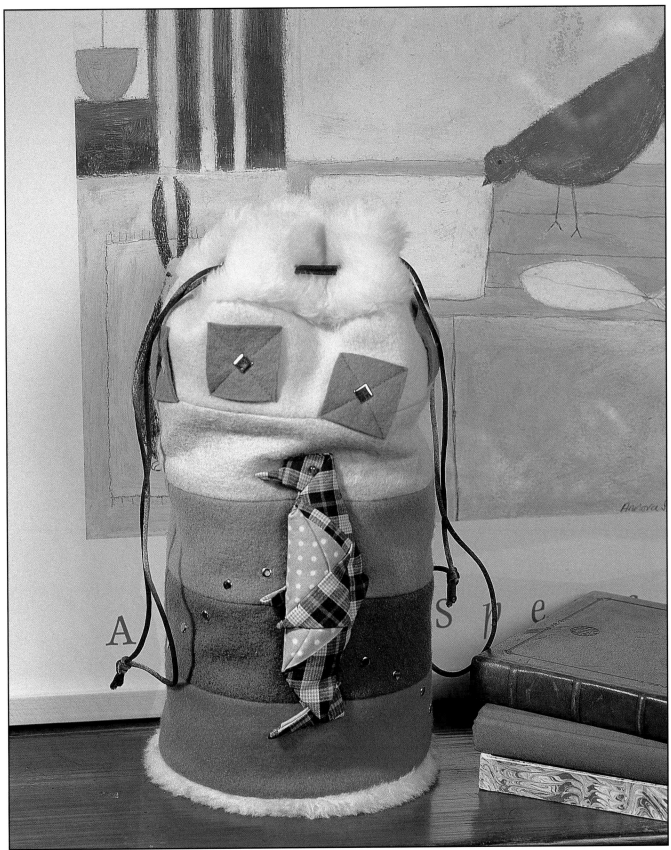

117

Continued from page 116.

6. Slip lining into tote tube, wrong sides facing. Pin tote to lining along upper and lower edges.

7. Layer wool and lining Base pieces, wrong sides facing. With lining side of Base facing lining side of tote body, pin and sew Base to tote lower edge, using ½" seam allowance. Sew again ⅛" inward from first stitched row. Trim seam allowance just past stitching. Press. Note: This seam is visible from the Tote right side.

8. Align and sew short ends of 1¼" x 17½" strip of faux fur, using ½" seam allowance. Bind Base seam with this strip. Sew short ends of 4" x 17½" piece of faux fur, right sides facing, using ½" seam allowance. Finger-press seam allowance open. Bind upper edge of tote with this piece.

## MAKING THE HANDLE

1. Mark center of upper binding into ten equally spaced 1⅝" intervals. Attach a grommet at each mark.

2. Cut satin cord in half. Slip one cord through grommet from one side of tote. Tie ends together. Repeat with second cord from opposite side of tote. Tie ends together. Pull on cords to close tote.

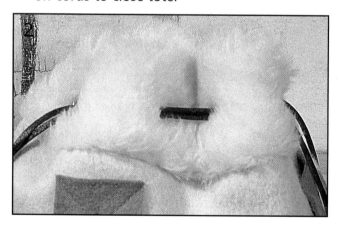

3. Slip piece of cardboard into tote at bottom.

## MAKING THE PENGUIN

1. Align 7½" edge of black plaid cotton piece with 7½" edge of light blue dot piece, right sides facing.

2. Sew edges together on both sides, using ¼" seam allowance and leaving a 1" opening along one seam. Press seam allowances open. See **Penguin** on page 119. Follow Steps 1–9. Fold one penguin.

3. Stitch bead onto face.

4. Stitch penguin onto tote. Note: The penguin is facing left.

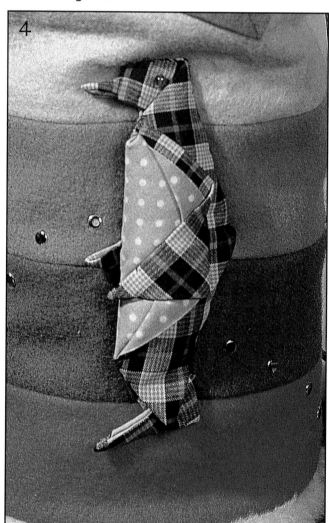

# FOLDING TECHNIQUE DIRECTIONS

## PENGUIN

  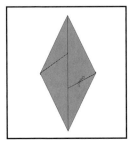 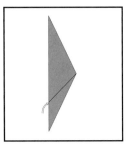

1. Position smaller-sized piece centered between larger piece, aligning raw end edges. Sew ends, using ¼" seam allowance. Trim bulk at corners and edge-press seam allowance.

2. Turn piece right side out through seam opening. Press well. See **Elephant** on page 107. Follow Steps 3–4.

3. Lift corner that is underneath fold from **Elephant** on page 107. Follow Step 4. Pull corner out to the right. Flatten and press. Repeat with remaining underneath corner.

4. Press piece in half and position flaps (flap will be penguin wing) downward. Repeat on other side.

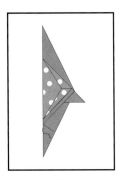 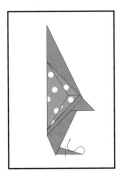 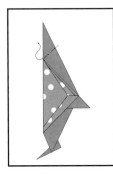 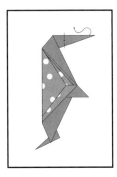 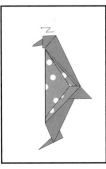

5. Pull flap outward to the right and position as shown. Flatten and press. Repeat on other side.

6. For foot, take lower tip to the right with inside reverse fold.

7. Fold lower right tip to the left with an opposite inside reverse fold.

8. For head, take upper tip to the right with an inside reverse fold.

9. Fold upper-right tip to the left with opposite inside reverse fold and make a stair-step fold within tip, forming beak.

# FLAMINGOS & DAISY PETAL TOTE

## FABRICS:

Note: All fabrics are a minimum of 36" wide.

### Ivory (two variations)
- Ivory/gold striped flannel (¼ yd) for tote Front, Back, and lining
- Ivory chenille (2" x 12") for binding

### Raspberry (four variations)
- Dark raspberry flannel (¼ yd) for petal backs and handle
- Dark raspberry plaid (¼ yd) for flamingo body
- Two variations of off-white/raspberry print (¼ yd each) for flamingo neck and head

### Yellow (one variation)
- Light yellow fabric (¼ yd) for petal fronts

## NOTIONS:

- **Standard Notions & Tools** on page 8
- 4mm plum round beads (2)
- Assorted red buttons (6)
- Fray preventative
- Matching threads
- Polyester stuffing (handful)

## PREPARING THE PIECES

Note: Enlarge patterns 200% unless otherwise indicated.

1. Using **Tote** pattern on page 125, cut Tote Front, Back, and Lining pieces from stripe flannel fabric. Note: This is four cuts from the same pattern.

2. Using **Flower Petal** pattern on page 124, cut five petals from each of the following fabrics:

- dark raspberry flannel
- yellow fabric

3. Cut two 1⅛" x 40" strips from dark raspberry flannel for handle.

4. Cut one 2" x 12" strip from ivory chenille for binding.

## ASSEMBLING THE TOTE

1. Place one yellow and one dark raspberry petal together, right sides facing. Stitch curved edges, leaving the straight edge unstitched. Trim bulk from tip and edge-press seam allowance open. Turn petal right side out and press well. Repeat with remaining petals.

2. Stitch Tote Front to Back along sides only, right sides facing, leaving opening on each side where indicated on the pattern. Press seam allowances open. Turn right side out. Repeat with Lining Front and Back, omitting side openings. Do not stitch bottom edges of Front/Back or Lining at this time. Press seam allowances open. Do not turn right side out.

3. Pin straight edge of petals to right side of Front between marks indicated on pattern. Note: The petals will overlap in order to fit the marked space. Baste-stitch in place ⅜" from top edge.

4. Slip Lining over Front/Back and petals, right sides facing, aligning upper edges and side seams. Sew upper edges together, using ½" seam allowance. Press seam allowance open, then flip lining to inside of Front/Back. Press upper edges. Topstitch close to seam and again ¾" from seam. At Front, fold upper edge down about ¾", causing petals to lay flat. Topstitch folded-over upper edge to the Front 1½" from each side seam. Pin lower edges together, then bind with chenille fabric strip.

## MAKING THE HANDLE

1. Press long edges of handle strips over ¼" to wrong side, then press piece in half again lengthwise.

2. Topstitch along both long edges. Slip one Handle through casing opening on one side of the bag, exiting at same opening. Tie ends together in a knot. Slip other Handle through casing opening on other side of bag in same manner. Tie ends together in a knot. Daub a bit of fray preventative onto Handle ends.

3. When dry, trim ends with a diagonal cut. Pull on both handles to close bag.

## MAKING THE FLAMINGO

1. Using **Flamingo Body** on page 125, cut body from dark raspberry plaid. Using **Flamingo**

**Head** pattern on page 124, cut one Head each from off-white/raspberry print fabrics.

2. Seam Bodies to Heads along diagonal edges right sides facing, using ¼" seam allowance. Press seam allowance open. See **Flamingo** below and on pages 123–124. Follow Steps 1–15. Make two flamingos.

3. Stitch one onto each face.

4. Stitch a portion of neck and body front and one leg onto tote front over center petals, having flamingos facing each other. Note: One flamingo faces left and the other, right.

5. Stitch one button onto tip of each petal and one between the two flamingos.

# FOLDING TECHNIQUE DIRECTIONS

## FLAMINGO

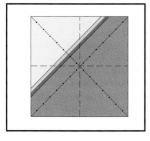

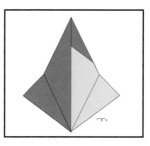

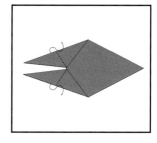

1. With fabric wrong side up, press piece in crosswise folds. With fabric right side up, press diagonally.

2. Collapse piece on folds to form Square Base. Be certain the pieced corner is positioned as shown.

3. Lift upper layer of bottom center corner upward while also folding outer edges inward to center. Press. Repeat on opposite side.

4. Position piece horizontally, with open "legs" pointing right. Flip bottom center up-ward to top center. Repeat on opposite side. This will reposition legs so they now point left.

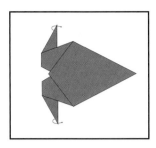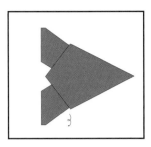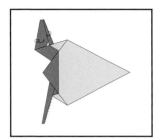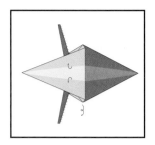

5. With contrasting corner facing down, fold each leg outward in an inside reverse fold.

6. Open out legs so that raw edges along leg centers are facing downward. Press leg tips under ¼".

7. Turn piece over. Fold upper edge of one leg two times so it is centered. Note: This is done within a layer of folds and is a bit tricky. Fold lower edge of leg two times to center, then once more so it is on top of upper fold. Stitch, finishing one leg. Repeat for other side.

8. Lift tip of upper triangle layer and pull it toward the left, exposing center raw edges. Press raw edges under. Reposition large triangles.

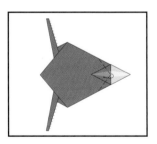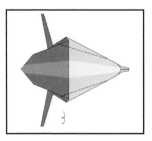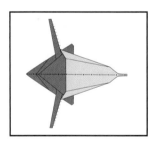

9. Turn piece over so that contrasting corner is facing downward. Press right tip of upper layer over as shown.

10. Press upper- and lower-right corners of upper layer to center. Tack to hold.

11. Press upper layer to left along widest section. Press right tip of contrasting corner over ¼", then fold tip edges together and whipstitch for a space of ½".

12. Turn piece over. Press top and bottom edges of contrasting tip as shown.

Continued on page 124.

Continued from page 124.

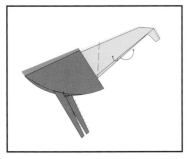 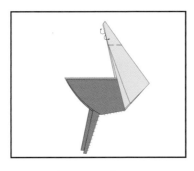 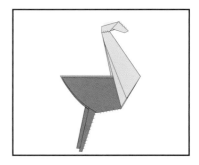

13. Fold piece in half.

14. Tuck center bottom points under and within flamingo body, tack to hold. Make an outside reverse fold with neck piece (contrasting fabric).

15. Make another outside reverse fold with tip of neck piece to form beak. Tack head/beak in place. Tack neck to body.

## FLAMINGO & DAISY PETAL TOTE PATTERNS

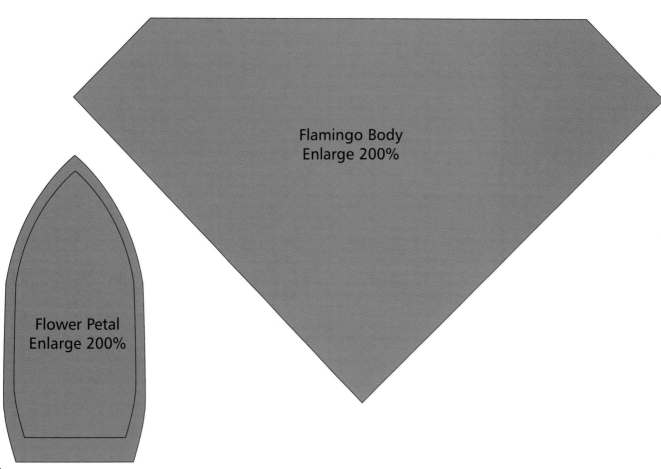

Flamingo Body
Enlarge 200%

Flower Petal
Enlarge 200%

# FLAMINGO & DAISY PETAL TOTE PATTERNS

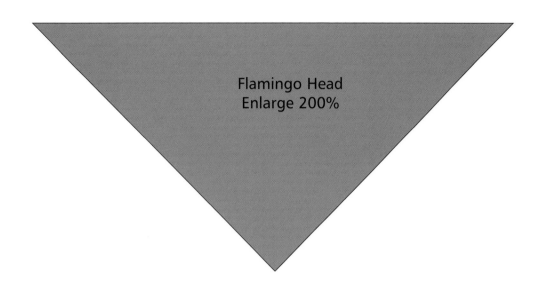

Flamingo Head
Enlarge 200%

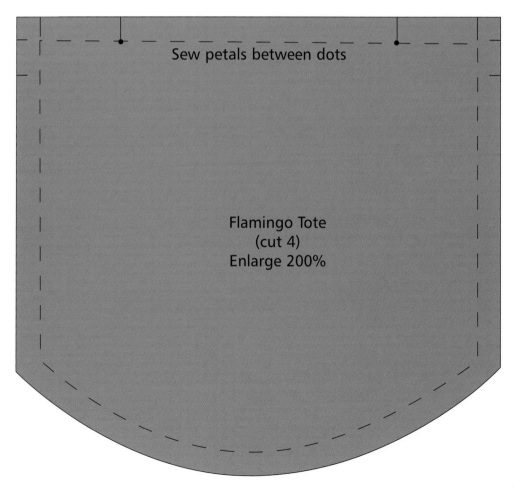

Sew petals between dots

Flamingo Tote
(cut 4)
Enlarge 200%

# ABOUT THE AUTHOR

Mary Jo Hiney has been an author with Sterling/Chapelle since 1992 and this book is her 16th offering in collaboration with the teams at Sterling Publishing and Chapelle, Ltd,.—opportunities for which she is filled with gratitude. As a freelance designer, Mary Jo also contributes her design skills to other enterprises in the fabric and craft industry, including her own.

Mary Jo has a love for fabric and sewing that she credits to her mom, when, as a child, together they would visit the local fabric store and savor the loveliness in each bolt of fabric and the excitement for the project in mind. Mary Jo was taught the art of quilting by her sister, Rose, who continues to inspire her and with whom she can discuss ideas and get excellent creative advice. Mary Jo lives with her family on the treasured Central Coast of California.

## DEDICATION

For Josh, to commemorate your graduation from California Polytechnic State University, San Luis Obispo, and to the hope that is within your life.

## ACKNOWLEDGMENTS

Although this book bears my name on the front cover, it is with the help of many devoted people that a project like this, from the beginning of the concept to the delivery of the finished product, comes to fruition. I would like to acknowledge the dedicated work of my friends at Chapelle, Ltd,. who have given of themselves on my behalf so lovingly for the past 12 years. It has been my privilege to be a part of the team all these years. For this project, I want to express my gratitude to my editor, Karmen, for creating a clear and lovely manner in which to convey the art of Quiltagami. Karmen has painstakingly and artfully organized the information, pouring through each page over and again to make certain everything has been correctly represented. I also want to thank Kim for her exceptional diagrams, because I have complete confidence in them and I know they will stand the test of time.

# METRIC CONVERSION CHARTS

## mm-millimetres cm-centimetres
### inches to millimetres and centimetres

| inches | mm | cm | inches | cm | inches | cm |
|---|---|---|---|---|---|---|
| $\frac{1}{8}$ | 3 | 0.3 | 9 | 22.9 | 30 | 76.2 |
| $\frac{1}{4}$ | 6 | 0.6 | 10 | 25.4 | 31 | 78.7 |
| $\frac{3}{8}$ | 10 | 1.0 | 11 | 27.9 | 32 | 81.3 |
| $\frac{1}{2}$ | 13 | 1.3 | 12 | 30.5 | 33 | 83.8 |
| $\frac{5}{8}$ | 16 | 1.6 | 13 | 33.0 | 34 | 86.4 |
| $\frac{3}{4}$ | 19 | 1.9 | 14 | 35.6 | 35 | 88.9 |
| $\frac{7}{8}$ | 22 | 2.2 | 15 | 38.1 | 36 | 91.4 |
| 1 | 25 | 2.5 | 16 | 40.6 | 37 | 94.0 |
| $1\frac{1}{4}$ | 32 | 3.2 | 17 | 43.2 | 38 | 96.5 |
| $1\frac{1}{2}$ | 38 | 3.8 | 18 | 45.7 | 39 | 99.1 |
| $1\frac{3}{4}$ | 44 | 4.4 | 19 | 48.3 | 40 | 101.6 |
| 2 | 51 | 5.1 | 20 | 50.8 | 41 | 104.1 |
| $2\frac{1}{2}$ | 64 | 6.4 | 21 | 53.3 | 42 | 106.7 |
| 3 | 76 | 7.6 | 22 | 55.9 | 43 | 109.2 |
| $3\frac{1}{2}$ | 89 | 8.9 | 23 | 58.4 | 44 | 111.8 |
| 4 | 102 | 10.2 | 24 | 61.0 | 45 | 114.3 |
| $4\frac{1}{2}$ | 114 | 11.4 | 25 | 63.5 | 46 | 116.8 |
| 5 | 127 | 12.7 | 26 | 66.0 | 47 | 119.4 |
| 6 | 152 | 15.2 | 27 | 68.6 | 48 | 121.9 |
| 7 | 178 | 17.8 | 28 | 71.1 | 49 | 124.5 |
| 8 | 203 | 20.3 | 29 | 73.7 | 50 | 127.0 |

## yards to metres

| yards | metres | yards | metres | yards | metres | yards | metres | yards | metres |
|---|---|---|---|---|---|---|---|---|---|
| $\frac{1}{8}$ | 0.11 | $2\frac{1}{8}$ | 1.94 | $4\frac{1}{8}$ | 3.77 | $6\frac{1}{8}$ | 5.60 | $8\frac{1}{8}$ | 7.43 |
| $\frac{1}{4}$ | 0.23 | $2\frac{1}{4}$ | 2.06 | $4\frac{1}{4}$ | 3.89 | $6\frac{1}{4}$ | 5.72 | $8\frac{1}{4}$ | 7.54 |
| $\frac{3}{8}$ | 0.34 | $2\frac{3}{8}$ | 2.17 | $4\frac{3}{8}$ | 4.00 | $6\frac{3}{8}$ | 5.83 | $8\frac{3}{8}$ | 7.66 |
| $\frac{1}{2}$ | 0.46 | $2\frac{1}{2}$ | 2.29 | $4\frac{1}{2}$ | 4.11 | $6\frac{1}{2}$ | 5.94 | $8\frac{1}{2}$ | 7.77 |
| $\frac{5}{8}$ | 0.57 | $2\frac{5}{8}$ | 2.40 | $4\frac{5}{8}$ | 4.23 | $6\frac{5}{8}$ | 6.06 | $8\frac{5}{8}$ | 7.89 |
| $\frac{3}{4}$ | 0.69 | $2\frac{3}{4}$ | 2.51 | $4\frac{3}{4}$ | 4.34 | $6\frac{3}{4}$ | 6.17 | $8\frac{3}{4}$ | 8.00 |
| $\frac{7}{8}$ | 0.80 | $2\frac{7}{8}$ | 2.63 | $4\frac{7}{8}$ | 4.46 | $6\frac{7}{8}$ | 6.29 | $8\frac{7}{8}$ | 8.12 |
| 1 | 0.91 | 3 | 2.74 | 5 | 4.57 | 7 | 6.40 | 9 | 8.23 |
| $1\frac{1}{8}$ | 1.03 | $3\frac{1}{8}$ | 2.86 | $5\frac{1}{8}$ | 4.69 | $7\frac{1}{8}$ | 6.52 | $9\frac{1}{8}$ | 8.34 |
| $1\frac{1}{4}$ | 1.14 | $3\frac{1}{4}$ | 2.97 | $5\frac{1}{4}$ | 4.80 | $7\frac{1}{4}$ | 6.63 | $9\frac{1}{4}$ | 8.46 |
| $1\frac{3}{8}$ | 1.26 | $3\frac{3}{8}$ | 3.09 | $5\frac{3}{8}$ | 4.91 | $7\frac{3}{8}$ | 6.74 | $9\frac{3}{8}$ | 8.57 |
| $1\frac{1}{2}$ | 1.37 | $3\frac{1}{2}$ | 3.20 | $5\frac{1}{2}$ | 5.03 | $7\frac{1}{2}$ | 6.86 | $9\frac{1}{2}$ | 8.69 |
| $1\frac{5}{8}$ | 1.49 | $3\frac{5}{8}$ | 3.31 | $5\frac{5}{8}$ | 5.14 | $7\frac{5}{8}$ | 6.97 | $9\frac{5}{8}$ | 8.80 |
| $1\frac{3}{4}$ | 1.60 | $3\frac{3}{4}$ | 3.43 | $5\frac{3}{4}$ | 5.26 | $7\frac{3}{4}$ | 7.09 | $9\frac{3}{4}$ | 8.92 |
| $1\frac{7}{8}$ | 1.71 | $3\frac{7}{8}$ | 3.54 | $5\frac{7}{8}$ | 5.37 | $7\frac{7}{8}$ | 7.20 | $9\frac{7}{8}$ | 9.03 |

# INDEX